New York, New York   Columbus, Ohio   Chicago, Illinois   Peoria, Illinois   Woodland Hills, California

Illustrators: *Gregory Benton, Ariel Bordeaux, Jim Callahan, Mark Carolan, Greg Lawhun, Pat Lewis, Ellen Lindner, Mitch O'Connell, John Pham, Joel Priddy, Brian Ralph, Scott Rolfs, and Rob Ullman*

The McGraw-Hill Companies

Send all inquiries to:

Glencoe/McGraw-Hill
8787 Orion Place
Columbus, OH 43240-4027

ISBN-13: 978-0-07-874737-3
ISBN-10: 0-07-874737-6

Printed in the United States of America.

8 9 10 045 10 09 08

TABLE OF CONTENTS

THEME 9

THEME 10

THEME 11

THEME 12

THEME 13

USING GRAPHIC NOVELS:

POPULAR CULTURE AND SOCIAL STUDIES INTERACT

Graphic novels represent a significant segment of the literary market for adolescents and young adults. These stories may resemble comic books, but on closer inspection, they often address controversial issues using complex story lines. Some graphic novels that are well known to Western audiences are *Watchmen,* which examines how superheroes live in a society that has turned against them; *Maus,* which uses anthropomorphic characters to tell the story of a Holocaust survivor; *From Hell,* which presents one explanation for the actions of the historical serial killer Jack the Ripper; and *Road to Perdition,* which was made into a popular motion picture.

WHAT ARE GRAPHIC NOVELS?

Graphic novels, as they are known in Western countries, were initially inspired by Japanese *manga* (comics) and *anime* (animation). *Anime* style is most commonly recognizable in its use of large-eyed characters with oversized heads, and it has increasingly been recognized by Western audiences as a distinct art form.

Use of the *manga* genre in Japan is far more widespread than in Western countries and dates back to the early part of the twentieth century. Japanese *manga,* rendered in black and white and printed on newsprint, are read by children and adults and include many topics, although science fiction *mechas* (robots) dominate the field. The topics of these works are surprisingly similar to Western young adult fiction. A large portion of the market is *shojo,* comic books designed to appeal to girls. A popular *shojo* character that appears in America is the *Sailor Moon* series, featuring a resourceful Japanese schoolgirl. *Shonen manga* is designed primarily for boys and usually consists of action stories. Teachers may recognize elements of *shonen manga* in Japanese game cards collected and traded by many American youth. Many *manga* are published in serial form in books as long as 750 pages. One of the first *manga* marketed for Western consumption was *The Four Immigrants Manga: A Japanese Experience in San Francisco, 1904–1924* (Kiyama, 1999), first published in 1931. It is not in the *anime* style of today's novels, but offers a poignant portrayal of the challenges facing Asian immigrants at the time.

Why Do Graphic Novels Appeal to Students?

Part of the appeal of graphic novels lies in their "underground" (and therefore forbidden) reputation. Another part of the appeal of *manga* and *anime* lies in their sophisticated story lines and the development of complex characters (Izawa, 2002). Unlike American comic books that feature a superhero with fixed and exaggerated attributes, many of these Japanese stories include a subtext of universal themes involving ethical and moral dilemmas. These *gekiga* (literary novels) are ambitious in their scope and intricacy and are becoming more available in English translations. Unlike the broad range of stories available in Japan, however, the stream of *manga* and *anime* reaching Western readers is not so diverse. The bulk of *manga* and *anime* available in America are often skewed toward violent and sexually graphic titles (called *hentai,* or "perverse"), which do not reflect the wide range of quality available.

Graphic novels continue to develop and diversify (Frey & Fisher, 2004). Interactive graphic novels presented in serial form are appearing on the Internet. Readers have a number of options when they visit the site each month to view the next installment, such as engaging in role-playing games, creating new characters to interact with those developed by the author, and visiting an extensive catalog for background information. Most of these Web-based graphic novels have decidedly adult content, although users are likely to be Web-savvy adolescents. A unique subset of these graphic novels and *manga* is a style of writing called *fanfiction,* in which readers create and post their own alternative versions of stories featuring their favorite characters (e.g., Chandler-Olcott & Mahar, 2003).

Why Use Graphic Novels in Social Studies?

Graphic novels are amazingly diverse, in terms of both their content and their usefulness. For example, Gorman (2002) notes that graphic novels are exactly what teens are looking for: they are motivating, engaging, challenging, and interesting. Schwartz (2002b, 2004) believes that graphic novels are engaging because they allow teachers to enter the youth culture and students to bring their "out of school" experiences into the classroom. The purpose of such **"multiple literacies"** is to bridge the gap between students' school literacy and the ways in which they use reading and writing outside of school.

Graphic novels have also been used effectively with students with disabilities, students who struggle with reading, and English learners (e.g., Cary, 2004; Frey & Fisher, 2004; Schwartz, 2002a). One of the theories behind the use of graphic novels for struggling adolescent readers focuses on their effectiveness in presenting complex ideas while reducing the reading demands. As a result, all students can thoughtfully discuss the content at hand. As Weiner (2003) noted,

> Graphic novels have found their way into the classroom, as teachers are realizing their usefulness as literacy tools. After a study of graphic novels, researchers concluded that the average graphic novel introduced readers to twice as many words as the average children's book. This realization has reinforced the idea that the comics format is a good way to impart information. (p. 61)

Conclusions

While controversy about graphic novels persists—especially among people who worry that graphic novels will bring the end of traditional books—our experiences with adolescents, as well as a number of current research studies, suggest that graphic novels are an important adjunct in our instruction. Graphic novels are viable options for students with disabilities, struggling readers, and English learners, but they are more powerful than that. Graphic novels are motivating and engaging for all students. They allow us to differentiate our instruction and provide universal access to the curriculum. We hope you'll find the graphic novels in this book useful as you engage your students in the study of history and social studies.

Sincerely,

Douglas Fisher & Nancy Frey

Douglas Fisher, Ph.D.
Professor
San Diego State University

Nancy Frey, Ph.D.
Assistant Professor
San Diego State University

REFERENCES

Cary, S. (2004). *Going graphic: Comics at work in the multilingual classroom.* Portsmouth, NH: Heinemann.

Chandler-Olcott, K., & Mahar, D. (2003). Adolescents' anime-inspired "fanfictions": An exploration of multiliteracies. *Journal of Adolescent & Adult Literacy,* 46, 556–566.

Fisher, D., & Frey, N. (2004). *Improving adolescent literacy: Strategies at work.* Upper Saddle River, NJ: Merrill Education.

Frey, N., & Fisher, D. (2004). Using graphic novels, anime, and the Internet in an urban high school. *English Journal, 93*(3), 19–25.

Gorman, M. (2002). What teens want: Thirty graphic novels you can't live without. *School Library Journal, 48*(8) 42–47.

Izawa, E. (2004). *What are manga and anime?* Retrieved December 5, 2004, from www.mit.edu:8001/people/rei/Expl.html.

Kiyama, H. Y. (1999). *The four immigrants manga: A Japanese experience in San Francisco, 1904–1924.* Berkeley, CA: Stone Bridge Press.

Schwarz, G. (2002a). Graphic books for diverse needs: Engaging reluctant and curious readers. *ALAN Review, 30*(1), 54–57.

Schwarz, G. E. (2002b). Graphic novels for multiple literacies. *Journal of Adolescent & Adult Literacy, 46,* 262–265.

Schwarz, G. E. (2004). Graphic novels: Multiple cultures and multiple literacies. *Thinking Classroom, 5*(4), 17–24.

Weiner, S. (2003). *The rise of the graphic novel: Faster than a speeding bullet.* New York: Nantier Beall Minoustchine Publishing.

TEACHING STRATEGIES FOR GRAPHIC NOVELS

As we have noted, graphic novels are an excellent adjunct text. While they cannot and should not replace reading or the core, standards-based textbook, they can be used effectively to build students' background knowledge, to motivate students, to provide a different access route to the content, and to allow students to check and review their work.

Strategies for using graphic novels in the classroom include the following:

1. **Previewing Content.** In advance of the text reading, you can use a graphic novel as a way to activate background information and prior knowledge. For example, you may display a graphic novel on the overhead projector and discuss it with the class. Using a teacher think-aloud, in which you share your thinking about the graphic novel with the class, you might provide students with advance information that they will read later in the book. Alternatively, you may display the graphic novel and invite students, in pairs or groups, to share their thinking with one another. Regardless of the approach, the goal is to activate students' interest and background knowledge prior to the reading.

2. **Narrative Writing.** Ask students to read one of the graphic novels, paying careful attention to the details and imagery used. Then ask each student to write their own summary of the story being told in this novel. Graphic novels without much dialogue provide an opportunity for students to create their own dialogue, based on what they know of the content and character. Not only does this engage students in thinking about the content, it also provides you with some assessment information. Based on the dialogue that the students write, you'll understand what they already know, what they misunderstand from the story, and what they do not yet know.

3. **Summarizing Information.** A third possible use of graphic novels involves writing summaries. Like oral retellings of readings, written summaries require that students consider the main ideas in a piece of text and use their own words to recap what they know (Frey, Fisher, & Hernandez, 2003). Students can discuss the graphic novel and the text they've read with a small group, and then create their own summaries. Alternatively, students could summarize the text and then create a compare-and-contrast graphic organizer in which they note the differences between their summary of the text and the way that the author/illustrator of the graphic novel summarized the text (e.g., Fisher & Frey, 2004).

4 **Reviewing Content.** In addition to serving as fodder for written summaries, graphic novels can be used for review of content. While there are many reasons to review content—such as preparing for a test—graphic novels are especially useful for providing students with a review of past chapters. You can use a graphic novel from a previous chapter to review the major events in time or place, so that students can situate the new information they are reading in a context.

5 **Analysis.** Graphic novels often have a thematic strand that illustrates a specific point about the content being studied. This may take the form of irony, humor, or a more direct and formal approach to a historical event. In their analysis, students read the graphic novel with the intention of trying to understand the main point the author is trying to convey. This approach is particularly useful after students have covered the content in the main textbook. Encouraging students to pose questions about the text will help to uncover the main points.

For example:

- Why did the author choose this topic?
- What does this graphic novel tell me about the people we have studied? Does the story relate ideas about their society, culture, religion, government, military, or economy, to other aspects of their life?
- Is the tone of the story humorous or serious?
- Do I like the people being presented?
- Does the author portray the characters in a positive or negative way?
- What conclusions do these ideas suggest?

Have students write a few sentences answering these questions. Then have them summarize what they believe is the main point of the graphic novel.

6 **Visualizing.** Have students skim the chapter or a particular section of the chapter. Students should then pick one person, one event, or one concept from their reading and create their own graphic representation of it. Students could use a comic book style to illustrate their topic. Their work could be funny, sad, serious, satirical, or any other tone that they wish. They can use text and dialogue or let the pictures alone tell the story. Another option would be to use other media for their depiction of the topic. Students could take pictures, make a computer slide-show presentation, make a video, or create a song to represent their topic.

These are just some of the many uses of graphic novels. As you introduce them into your class, you may discover more ways to use this popular art form to engage your students in a new method of learning while exercising the multiple literacies your students already possess. We welcome you to the world of learning through graphic novels!

Fisher, D., & Frey, N. (2004). *Improving adolescent literacy: Strategies at work.* Upper Saddle River, NJ: Merrill Education.

Frey, N., Fisher, D., & Hernandez, T. (2003). "What's the gist?" Summary writing for struggling adolescent writers. *Voices from the Middle,* 11(2), 43–49.

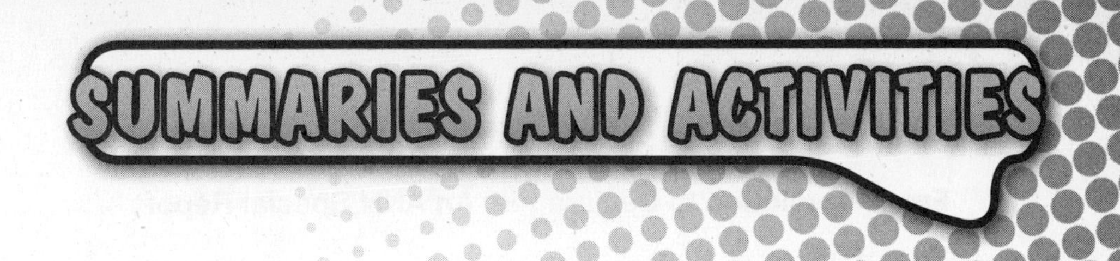

American History in Graphic Novel

The following pages contain additional information about each graphic novel. You will find background information, brief summaries of each graphic novel, and two activities to help you guide your students' understanding of each graphic novel. The first activity is designed to help the student utilize the story presented to complete the assigned task. The second activity is more broadly focused, allowing students to make connections between the graphic novel and the larger historical context of the period.

Theme 1, pages 1–6

**LCSI: Roanoke:
Lost Colony Scene Investigation**

Summary

The English colony of Roanoke was one of the earliest attempts to plant European settlers in the New World. Sir Walter Raleigh was granted a charter by Queen Elizabeth and in 1585 Raleigh sent about 100 men to settle an island in what is today North Carolina's Outer Banks. The colonists remained through a difficult winter and returned to England in the spring. Two years later, Raleigh sent 91 men, 17 women, and 9 children to the Roanoke location.

John White, the leader of the settlement, returned to England after a month for more supplies. However, war between England and Spain prevented White from returning for almost three years. When he was able to return, the colony was deserted. The houses were empty and no sign of the colonists remained except a wooden post with carvings possibly referring to the Croatoans or Native Americans living nearby. The circumstances of the disappearance of the "Lost Colony" remain a mystery.

The graphic novel begins at this point. The Lost Colony Scene Investigation team has come to Roanoke to find clues to determine what might have happened to the missing colonists.

Activities

1. Have students visualize what happened to the Roanoke settlers. Divide the class into groups of three or four students and ask each group to write a play describing its theory of what happened to the colonists. If time permits, have each group perform its play for the class.
2. Ask students to review the section entitled "English Colonies in America" in the textbook chapter on colonization. Have students explain how the Roanoke colony was to aid England in the fight against Spain.

Theme 2, pages 7–12

From Revolution to Declaration: An ANN Special Report

Summary

Great Britain faced an enormous financial debt following the French and Indian War. New tax policies for the American colonies were devised to help pay for the 10,000 British soldiers stationed in North America. Chancellor of the Exchequer George Grenville of Great Britain and the British Parliament began by strictly enforcing customs duties and introducing new taxes to increase revenue.

American merchants protested that Parliament could not tax the colonies for the purpose of raising money—only to regulate trade. Britain placed customs duties on many goods, including glass, lead, paper, paint, and tea, imported into the colonies. Angry colonists attacked British customs officers in the colonies. On March 5, 1770, crowds began taunting and throwing snowballs at a British soldier guarding the customs house in Boston. A group of soldiers came to his aid and began firing into the crowd, killing five and wounding six colonists. The shootings became known as the Boston Massacre. A few weeks later, news arrived that Britain had repealed almost all of the customs duties except the tax on tea. The repeal brought only temporary peace.

On September 5, 1774, the First Continental Congress met in Philadelphia to discuss further action to address the division between Great Britain and the colonies. The Declaration of Rights and Grievances announced the formation of a nonimportation association and called for every county and town to form committees to enforce a boycott of British goods. The delegates agreed to hold a Second Continental Congress in May 1775 if the disagreements continued.

When the Second Continental Congress met in Philadelphia in May, British soldiers and colonial militia had already battled in Lexington and Concord. The Congress voted to form the Continental Army and appointed George Washington as general and commander in chief of the new army in June 1775.

In early July, a committee composed of leaders such as John Adams, Benjamin Franklin, and Thomas Jefferson submitted the Declaration of Independence to the Continental Congress, declaring the colonies the United States of America and asserting their independence from Britain. The American Revolution had officially begun.

In this story, the American News Network (ANN) makes a broadcast on July 4, 1776, covering the events leading up to the signing of the Declaration of Independence, complete with eyewitness accounts and up-to-the-minute coverage.

Activities

1. Have students use library and Internet resources to research the terms of the Coercive Acts. Have students take the point of view of an eyewitness to some of the "intolerable" laws imposed upon colonists and write an eyewitness account for the ANN broadcast.

2. Have students create a flow chart for the Revolutionary War showing the cause and effect relationships among the events leading up to the signing of the Declaration of Independence.

Theme 3, pages 13–19

The Seneca Falls Convention

Summary

The Seneca Falls Convention was organized by antislavery activists Lucretia Mott and Elizabeth Cady Stanton in July 1848 to discuss women's rights. In order to define the women's goals, Stanton wrote a speech to capture exactly what the women hoped to accomplish.

The Seneca Falls Declaration of Sentiments and Resolutions, as it became known, drew its language and intent from the Declaration of Independence. The document declared that "all men and women are created equal" and instead of listing charges against the King of England, it leveled its charges against men.

The document also contained a list similar to the Bill of Rights that guaranteed rights for women, including the right to vote. Although only a few hundred people attended the convention, it was given a great deal of media attention and the Declaration was even printed in its entirety by the *New York Herald.*

Abolitionist Frederick Douglass attended the convention and was integral in getting the idea of women's voting rights approved by the convention delegates. Douglass stressed that women were entitled to the same basic rights men enjoyed. This convention is considered to be the unofficial beginning of the woman suffrage movement.

This graphic novel depicts Elizabeth Cady Stanton finding the inspiration to write the Declaration of Sentiments and Resolutions. When she shares her idea of giving women the right to vote with people who are close to her, they tell her it is ridiculous and unnatural. Stanton writes to Frederick Douglass in the hopes that he, of all people, will support her at the Seneca Falls Convention. When others scoff at her, Douglass defends Stanton's declaration that every citizen should have the right to vote.

Activities

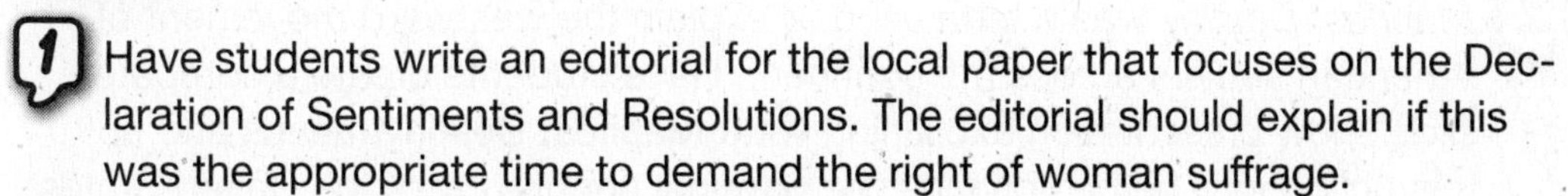

1. Have students write an editorial for the local paper that focuses on the Declaration of Sentiments and Resolutions. The editorial should explain if this was the appropriate time to demand the right of woman suffrage.

2. Reform movements of the mid-1800s targeted aspects of American society in need of change. Have students research a reform movement associated with this time period. Students should create posters or pamphlets encouraging people to support their cause.

Theme 4, pages 21–26

"Westward, Ho!"

Summary

In the mid-1800s, many Americans traveled west across the Great Plains to try prospecting gold in California, to spread their religious faith, or to own their own land. By 1820 2.4 million people lived west of the Appalachian Mountains. Most settled east of the Mississippi River, while more than 250,000 Americans headed west to California and the Pacific Northwest, traveling across the Great Plains and Rocky Mountains.

By the 1840s, several east-to-west passages played a vital role in the development of western settlements. Popular trails included the Oregon Trail, California Trail, and Santa Fe Trail. Emigrants traveled in trains of covered wagons.

Travelers feared attacks by Native Americans, though they rarely occurred. Those who did meet Native Americans were often offered gifts of food and information on routes, edible plants, and sources of water. Native Americans sometimes offered fresh horses to the emigrants in exchange for cotton clothing and ammunition. As the number of travelers on the trails increased, however, Native Americans began to worry for their way of life.

This graphic novel's structure is similar to a reality show on TV. It is designed to show the difficulty of traveling west, including severe weather, dangerous rivers, and a lack of refuge in times of danger. The characters include two families who are crossing the Great Plains on their way to California in search of gold. Each family's ultimate goal is to successfully cross the Plains before the other family.

Activities

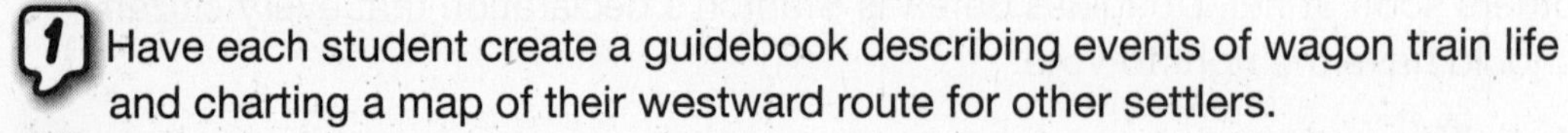

1. Have each student create a guidebook describing events of wagon train life and charting a map of their westward route for other settlers.

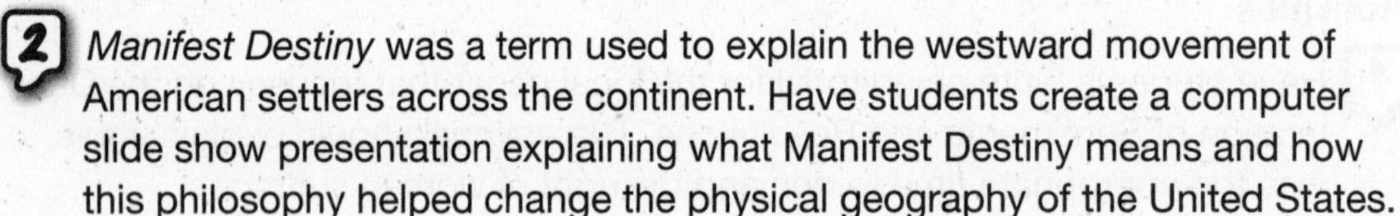

2. *Manifest Destiny* was a term used to explain the westward movement of American settlers across the continent. Have students create a computer slide show presentation explaining what Manifest Destiny means and how this philosophy helped change the physical geography of the United States.

Theme 5, pages 27–33

Fort Sumter's Last Stand

Summary

Some Southerners viewed the election of Abraham Lincoln in November 1860 as a threat to the Southern way of life. South Carolina, the location of Fort Sumter, was the first state to secede from the Union in December 1860.

In an effort to compromise, Senator John J. Crittenden of Kentucky proposed amendments to the Constitution in December 1860. The amendments would guarantee slavery where it already existed and reinstate the Missouri Compromise line, while extending it all the way to the California border. Slavery would be permitted south of the line, while it was prohibited north of the line. Crittenden's compromise effort was not successful.

By February 1, 1861, six states from the Lower South had seceded. A week later the seceding states declared themselves a new nation—the Confederate States of America. Jefferson Davis was selected to be president, and Confederate forces began seizing federal lands within the South. Fort Sumter, located in Charleston Harbor in South Carolina, remained occupied by Federal troops.

Lincoln stated in his inaugural address that he intended to "hold, occupy, and possess" federal property in seceded states. In April Lincoln announced he was going to resupply Fort Sumter. Davis decided the Confederacy should take Fort Sumter before the supply ship arrived. Confederate leaders delivered a note to Major Robert Anderson demanding Fort Sumter's surrender by the morning of April 12, 1861. Major Anderson stood his ground and the Confederate forces bombarded Fort Sumter for 33 hours before Major Anderson finally surrendered.

This story is told from the perspective of the wife of a U.S. Army officer stationed at Fort Sumter. She is reading a letter written by her husband describing the events at the fort in the weeks leading up to the bombardment.

Activities

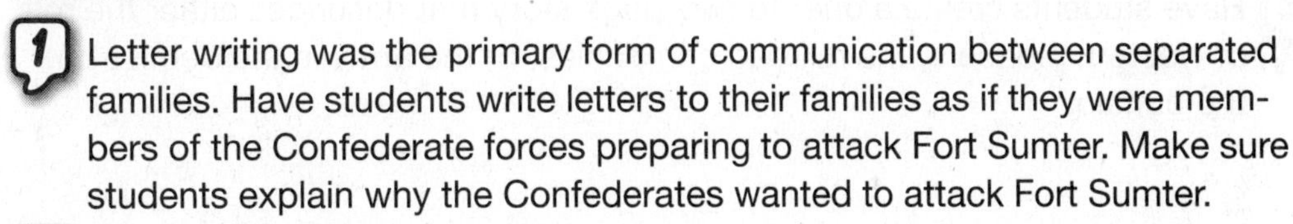

1. Letter writing was the primary form of communication between separated families. Have students write letters to their families as if they were members of the Confederate forces preparing to attack Fort Sumter. Make sure students explain why the Confederates wanted to attack Fort Sumter.

2. As states in the Lower South seceded, Congress tried to find a compromise to save the Union. Have students explain Crittenden's Compromise and why it did not succeed.

Theme 6, pages 35–39

The Importance of the Buffalo

Summary

By the 1870s, the great herds of buffalo, also known as the American bison, were rapidly disappearing. Millions of buffalo once roamed in the vast grasslands between the Rocky Mountains and the Mississippi River. The buffalo population began to decline as the numbers of American settlers pushed west across the Mississippi River to establish new cities and towns. One estimate states that in the mid-1850s there were approximately 20 million buffalo on the Plains, but by 1895 less than 1,000 remained. Western settlers killed thousands while crossing the Plains. Professional buffalo hunters killed the animals to sell the hides in eastern markets. Some hunters killed the buffalo for sport while others were hired by railroad companies to eliminate the buffalo from obstructing the rail lines. The United States Army also encouraged buffalo hunting as a means of forcing Native Americans onto reservations.

This graphic novel shows the importance of the buffalo to the Native Americans living on the Great Plains and how the loss of the buffalo population, combined with permanent American settlement, forced these Native American groups to make a choice—whether to continue to hold onto a cultural past that was changing or attempt to assimilate into the dominant culture. The novel begins in a classroom setting where the teacher is describing the challenges that the Native Americans faced resulting from dwindling buffalo numbers and cultural changes.

Activities

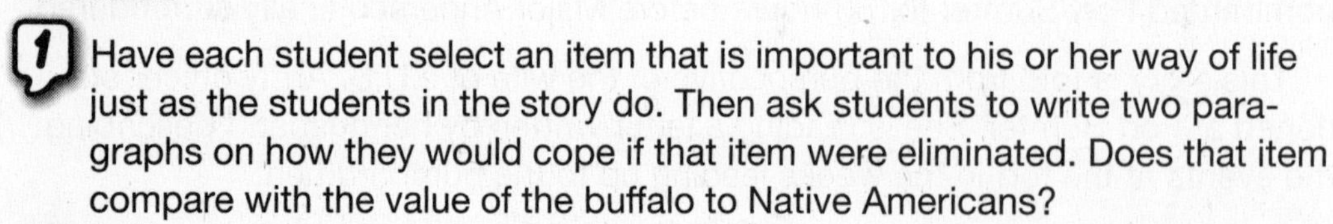

1. Have each student select an item that is important to his or her way of life just as the students in the story do. Then ask students to write two paragraphs on how they would cope if that item were eliminated. Does that item compare with the value of the buffalo to Native Americans?

2. Have students create a one- to two-page story that describes either the role of western pioneers, the railroad companies, or the army in the demise of the buffalo.

Theme 7, pages 41–44

Jeannette Rankin: First Woman in Congress

Summary

Jeannette Rankin was born June 11, 1880 in Missoula, Montana. She was the eldest of 11 children and spent most of her childhood on her family's ranch in Montana. In 1902 Rankin graduated from Montana State University with a degree in biology. She became involved in the woman suffrage movement at the University of Washington in 1910. Then she headed to New York to work for the National American Woman Suffrage Association (NAWSA) where she became its field secretary in 1912.

In 1913 Rankin, along with thousands of other suffragists, marched on Washington, D.C., prior to the inauguration of Woodrow Wilson to demand voting rights for women. Rankin then returned to Montana and gave up her position in NAWSA in order to help women from her home state gain suffrage. Montana granted women the right to vote in local and state elections in 1914.

Rankin ran as a Republican for a seat in the House of Representatives in 1916. She was a pacifist and wanted to keep the United States out of World War I. She won on an isolationist platform. As a representative, Rankin also sponsored legislation to grant federal voting rights and provide health services for women.

On April 4, 1917, shortly after Rankin joined Congress, President Woodrow Wilson actually misspoke when he addressed the body as "gentlemen of the Congress." Rankin was listening to President Wilson as he asked the legislature to declare war against Germany. Jeannette Rankin will be remembered for upholding her pacifist ideals by casting one of only 56 votes against U.S. entry into World War I, as well as the lone vote against declaring war against Japan in 1941.

This graphic novel tells the story of Jeannette Rankin's campaign for woman suffrage through the parades and protests she staged. As the first woman in Congress, she stands firm in her beliefs and votes against the U.S. entry into World War I.

Activities

1. Have students imagine that they are participating in a protest alongside Jeannette Rankin. Have them design banners and signs with slogans in favor of woman suffrage and create pamphlets or flyers outlining the reasons why women should be given the right to vote.
2. Jeannette Rankin was the first woman elected to the House of Representatives. Have students use library and Internet resources to research the first woman to serve and the first woman elected to the United States Senate. Have students create a brief biography of each woman.

Theme 8, pages 45–51

We're off to See the Pres

Summary

When Franklin Roosevelt was inaugurated in March 1933, the nation was deep in the Great Depression. One in four workers was unemployed and most of the nation's banks were closed. Between March 9 and June 16, 1933, Roosevelt requested and Congress passed 15 major acts. These acts and programs became known as the First New Deal.

Roosevelt's first action as president was to restore confidence in the banking system. Farms were also suffering due to high production and low demand. In order to save the farms, Roosevelt passed a bill that paid farmers not to grow certain overproduced crops. The program accomplished its goal: surplus declined and food prices and farm income increased. Bills were also passed that required industries to adhere to codes that limited the work week.

Rather than handing out money to the unemployed, Roosevelt felt that people needed the opportunity to earn their money. He created relief programs, such as the Civilian Conservation Corps, the Federal Emergency Relief Administration, the Public Works Administration, and the Civil Works Administration.

This graphic novel is about a little girl from a farming family in Kansas that is suffering from lack of demand for their crops. The girl is saddened by her family's troubles and one night dreams of traveling to Washington, D.C., to speak with the president. Along the way, the girl discovers that the entire nation is suffering from the Depression just like her own family. When she arrives at the White House, she meets others who are waiting to speak with Roosevelt as well. Together they explain their problems to the president and ask for his help. Roosevelt tells them that he has a plan that will solve their problems. When the girl wakes up, she tells her family that they have nothing to worry about, but the family has already heard that Roosevelt has begun his New Deal program.

Activities

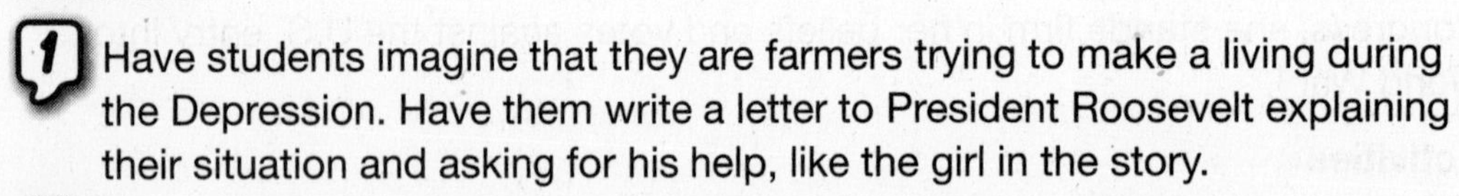

1. Have students imagine that they are farmers trying to make a living during the Depression. Have them write a letter to President Roosevelt explaining their situation and asking for his help, like the girl in the story.

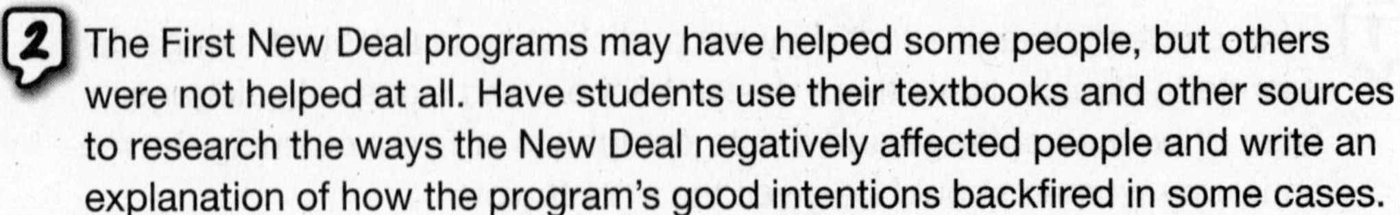

2. The First New Deal programs may have helped some people, but others were not helped at all. Have students use their textbooks and other sources to research the ways the New Deal negatively affected people and write an explanation of how the program's good intentions backfired in some cases.

Theme 9, pages 53–59

Seeking Shelter

Summary

The 1950s seemed to be a time of prosperity and security, especially when compared to the turmoil of the Great Depression and war of the previous two decades. This image, however, was flawed and incomplete. There were domestic issues and foreign tensions that affected the reality of the 1950s in important ways. One foreign tension, the fear of nuclear war, impacted the domestic perception of some American families. During the 1950s many Americans felt very uneasy about the threat of nuclear war. The nation was shocked when the Soviet Union successfully tested an atomic bomb in 1949. Americans prepared for the possibility of a nuclear attack in various ways. Schools conducted bomb preparation drills and set aside special areas as bomb shelters. Students were taught to "duck-and-cover" on the floor to protect themselves from the blasts. These precautions, however, would not protect them from fallout radiation left after the nuclear blast.

Perhaps the ultimate symbol of the fear of a nuclear attack was the fallout shelter, sometimes simply called a bomb shelter. While most cities and towns designated areas as community fallout shelters, some individuals felt that was not enough. To increase their chance of survival, some families built their own personal shelters in their backyards and basements. People stocked these fallout shelters with supplies such as canned foods, water, blankets, and a radio.

This graphic novel tells the story of a fallout shelter salesman and his quest to make the country safe, while also making a profit. His sales presentation is full of outrageous questions and equally outrageous claims about nuclear war.

Activities

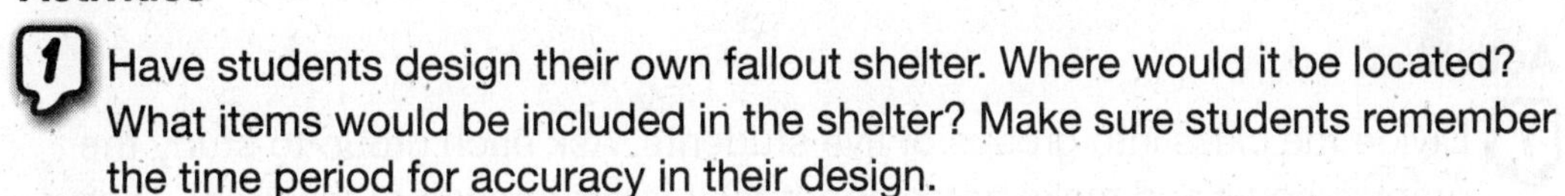
1 Have students design their own fallout shelter. Where would it be located? What items would be included in the shelter? Make sure students remember the time period for accuracy in their design.

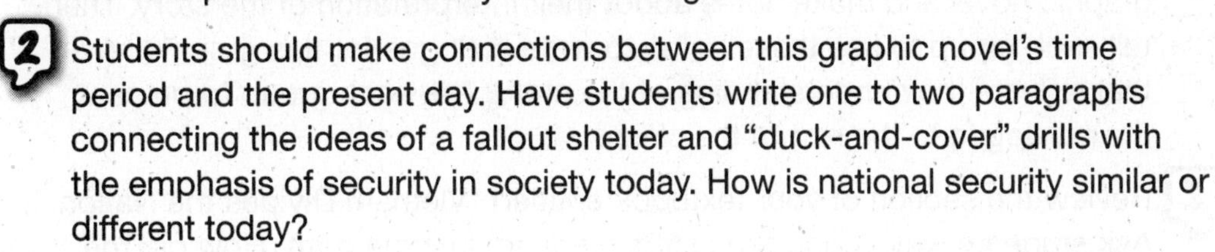
2 Students should make connections between this graphic novel's time period and the present day. Have students write one to two paragraphs connecting the ideas of a fallout shelter and "duck-and-cover" drills with the emphasis of security in society today. How is national security similar or different today?

Theme 10, pages 61–67

The Lottery

Summary

During the Vietnam War, the United States began a new method of drafting young men for military service. Previously, all men between the ages of 21 and 30 were required to register for the draft. A local draft board that consisted of civilians from local communities decided which individuals should be exempted from military service and which should be drafted.

As American military involvement in Vietnam escalated, officials increased the draft call. Many college students were now at risk of being drafted. An estimated 500,000 draftees refused to go, and angry draftees publicly burned draft cards, did not report for induction, or fled the country. Others decided to stay in the United States and face prosecution rather than fight in the war.

In 1969 the United States changed the method of drafting to a lottery system. Every day of the year was placed in a blue capsule, each day representing the potential draftee's birthday. The capsules were drawn one by one with each date assigned a draft number starting with one until each day had a number. Draftees were called for duty in order of their draft number until the military's needs were fulfilled. Individuals with lower lottery numbers were most likely to be called into service.

This graphic novel examines the effect of the draft lottery on two childhood friends. Each has registered with the Selective Service and they are watching the televised draft lottery together. One of the two friends receives a very high number, effectively protecting him from the draft. The other friend receives a low lottery number, making it very likely he will be drafted and sent to Vietnam. The results of the lottery determine very different lives for the young men.

Activities

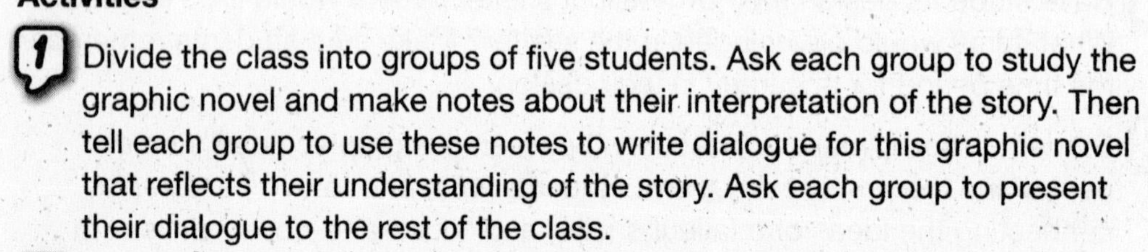

1. Divide the class into groups of five students. Ask each group to study the graphic novel and make notes about their interpretation of the story. Then tell each group to use these notes to write dialogue for this graphic novel that reflects their understanding of the story. Ask each group to present their dialogue to the rest of the class.

2. Review the section of your textbook entitled "Vietnam Divides the Nation." Ask students why young protesters were against the draft. How did the anger over the draft change voting rights?

Theme 11, pages 69–73

May Day

Summary

The United States was divided in opinion concerning the progress of the Vietnam War. Public support for the war began to drop and some Americans began to doubt the reassurances of the Johnson administration. Antiwar movements emerged as people began to protest publicly against the war and demand the United States pull out of Vietnam.

The protestors did not represent the majority opinion concerning Vietnam. Some Americans continued to support the war. Many of those individuals who supported the war criticized the protestors as being unpatriotic. By 1968 the nation seemed to be divided into two camps.

In 1968 Republican Richard Nixon won the election for president. He campaigned with promises to end the war and restore order at home. In August 1969, President Nixon's administration began secret peace talks with North Vietnam. He cut back the number of American troops in Vietnam but increased air strikes against North Vietnam and began bombing Vietcong sanctuaries in neighboring Cambodia.

In April 1970, President Nixon announced that American troops had invaded Cambodia in an effort to destroy Vietcong military bases. Many Americans viewed the invasion as a widening of the war and protests occurred. One such protest took place on May 4, 1970, at Kent State University in Ohio. The Ohio National Guard, armed with tear gas and rifles, fired upon the demonstrators. The soldiers fired without an order to do so and killed four students, wounding at least nine others.

This graphic novel tells the story of the shootings at Kent State by focusing on the mother of a college student attending the school. The mother is having coffee and discussing the protestors who are speaking out against the Vietnam War. Two women say the protestors are aiding the enemy and accuse them of being unpatriotic. The mother innocently mentions that her son is safe for now. Her son is going to college, which is how he has avoided being drafted.

Activities

This graphic novel is designed to avoid explicitly telling the students that the subject matter is the Kent State shootings. However, careful observation of the story's details provides enough clues that by the end of the graphic novel, the subject matter is clear. Ask students to review the novel and list the clues they find that indicate the story's purpose.

Have students explain in one to two paragraphs how the Vietnam War changed the office of the presidency.

Theme 12, pages 75–81

Life of Chad

Summary

The 2000 presidential election between Republican George W. Bush and Democrat Al Gore was one of the closest in U.S. history. Gore won the popular vote 48.4 percent to 47.9 percent. The state of Florida, with 25 electoral votes, was needed by each candidate to win the election. With the results extremely close, a recount using vote-counting machines was required by state law. However, thousands of votes had been thrown out because the counting machines could not discern a vote for president. Gore requested a hand recount of ballots in several strongly Democratic counties.

Bush held a slim lead following the machine recount and a battle emerged over the hand recounts. Most Florida ballots required voters to punch a hole in the ballot card—the cardboard punched out was called a chad. Difficulty emerged in the process of counting votes when the chad was still partially attached or not completely punched through. The complexity of the situation only increased because different counties used different standards to determine what the voter intended.

Time was another factor as a state law required the election results to be certified by a certain date. The Florida Supreme Court set a new deadline, but when the new deadline came the recounts were not complete. On November 26, 2000, Florida officials certified Bush the winner by 537 votes.

The Court battles continued with the Florida Supreme Court declaring the hand recounts should continue while the U.S. Supreme Court ordered the recount to stop. Finally, on December 12, the Supreme Court ruled in *Bush* v. *Gore* that the hand recounts in Florida violated the equal protection clause of the Fourteenth Amendment. Bush remained the certified winner in Florida and became the forty-third president of the United States.

This graphic novel focuses on the recount of the 2000 presidential election ballots in Florida. Elections officials are examining punch cards by holding them to the light and getting outside opinions on the validity of some questionable ballots. Some individuals are complaining about the Florida Supreme Court ruling that ordered the hand recounts of votes. Someone in the room notes the importance of this recounting, as the election is so close that even one vote could make a difference.

Activities

1. Hold a mock U.S. Supreme Court case or a panel discussion concerning *Bush* v. *Gore.* Divide students into the two sides and allow them time to prepare their arguments. Students should present written briefs detailing their opinions.

2. Have students research the local voting process for your county and state. What types of voting machines are used? What issues or problems may arise with these machines? Ask students if they think another voting method may be more effective.

Theme 13, pages 83–88

All Work and No Play

Summary

No single piece of technology has impacted U.S. culture in the late twentieth century more than the computer. Computers operate almost all pieces of technology today. The first computers of the 1950s were enormous machines. In 1959 Robert Noyce designed the first integrated circuit—a complete electronic circuit on a single chip of silicon—which made circuits smaller and easier to manufacture. In 1968 Intel revolutionized computers by combining several integrated circuits on a single chip. These microprocessors further reduced the size of computers and increased their speed.

In 1976 Stephen Wozniak and Steven Jobs founded Apple Computer and set out to build a computer for individual users. The following year they completed the first affordable home computer—the Apple II. In 1984 Apple created the Macintosh, which introduced the new concept of icons. Icons were on-screen graphic symbols that allowed users to access programs with the use of a hand-operated device called a mouse. International Business Machines (IBM) sparked by competition with Apple introduced a machine called the "Personal Computer," or PC, in 1981.

While Jobs and Wozniak were creating Apple, Bill Gates co-founded Microsoft to design PC software, the instructions used to program computers to perform desired tasks. In 1980 IBM hired Gates to develop an operating system for its new PC. The Windows operating system was introduced by Microsoft in 1985. Windows enabled the use of a mouse and on-screen graphics.

Computers have become essential tools in business and the world. People can communicate through electronic mail while using their home computers.

This graphic novel focuses on a hobbyist who spends considerable amounts of time improving computers in the 1970s. Meanwhile, another college student experiences trouble finishing a term paper and wishes there was a way to make writing term papers easier. In the end, the student finds out that while computers have brought about some important advances, these machines are not a guarantee against mistakes.

Activities

1. Computers have changed society in a variety of ways. Have students identify how society would be different without the use of computers. Would it make life simpler or more complex?

2. Have students write a brief one- to two-page biography about one of the leaders of the technological revolution.

THEME 1

Just ahead is our destination, Roanoke Island...where there should be 117 English settlers waiting to greet us.
Except that they've all disappeared.
ROANOKE ISLAND
ATLANTIC OCEAN
CROATAN SOUND
MAINLAND
LCSI:ROANOKE
LOST COLONY SCENE INVESTIGATION

On March 25, 1584 Queen Elizabeth I gave Walter Raleigh a six-year charter to explore, settle, and claim as his own any North American lands not already occupied by Europeans. Because of the danger and because he was a court favorite, Raleigh was allowed to organize and profit from, but not join personally, the expeditions to North America.
Almost without a trace.
How could 91 men, 17 women, and 9 children just disappear?
So we're here to search for clues to their whereabouts.
I'm sure Sir Walter Raleigh would like to know what happened. These were brave families who sold everything they owned in England to buy a share of Raleigh's holdings.
They wanted to settle near the deeper harbor of Chesapeake Bay, but ended up here at Roanoke instead, at the same place the first colony had been.
So this was actually the second settlement of Roanoke?
Yes, the first settlement attempt was all men, mostly soldiers, who barely made it through one winter and returned to England in the spring.
I heard they didn't get along too well with the local people.
In fact, the soldiers of the first settlement antagonized the native population with their constant demands for food and by spreading diseases for which they had no immunity. Even worse, mistrust led the soldiers to attack the Roanoke tribe, killing their chief and others.

In August, 1587, Governor John White boarded a ship bound for England to secure additional supplies for the colonists.
He hoped to be back by the following spring, but he didn't return until three years later in August, 1590.
So that was when the missing settlers were last seen?
LCSI
He got waylaid by war with the Spanish. Every ship was needed to fight off the Armada.
And this was all there was when he returned?
There were five chests of the Governors books and drawings that had been ripped apart and left out in the rain.
And a few iron cannonballs and rusty guns in the grass.
But no settlers, no boats, and no bodies. Hmmm...

EVIDENCE

Do you think the colonists might have starved to death?
It couldn't have been easy to grow enough food to make it through the winter.
Recent analysis of tree rings in the Roanoke Island area shows that it may have been impossible for the colonists to raise a corn crop. They had the misfortune of settling during the worst drought in 800 years.

There is no evidence **anywhere!** How could all those people disappear without a trace?
I found something down closer to the water... there's something carved in one of the ruins!
A message from the settlers?
Maybe, but it doesn't make much sense.

Weren't the colonists supposed to leave a message if they decided to move up the Chesapeake Bay?
Yes, or if they moved anywhere. And if they were in trouble, they were to add the shape of a cross to their message.
It doesn't sound like anything having to do with Chesapeake Bay.
But it could refer to the Croatoan Indians, or Croatoan Island to the south of here.
CRO
Well, no cross, but what does "C-R-O" mean?
The colonists were friendly with the Croatoans. Maybe they went to them for help
Strangely, no English people ever searched for the Roanoke colonists on Croatoan Island or the other areas where the Croatoan Indians lived. Governor White attempted to find them, but he was prevented by dangerous storms and forced to sail back to England. He never made another trip to America. Later, Jamestown colonists searched for the Roanoke settlers, but not in Croatoan territories.

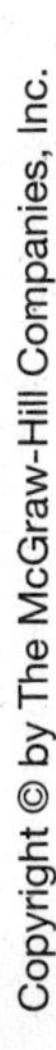

I guess we'll never know for sure what happened to the Lost Colony of Roanoke.

THE END ?

THEME 2

FROM REVOLUTION TO DECLARATION

IN CONGRESS, JULY 4, 1776.

The unanimous Declaration of the thirteen united States of America,

AN ANN SPECIAL REPORT

1776

ARE WE ON? HELLO?

TESTING, ONE, TWO, THREE...

WHAT'S THAT? WE'RE ON?

AHEM. GOOD EVENING, I'M JONATHAN WILLIAMS AND YOU ARE WATCHING THE INAUGURAL BROADCAST OF ANN, THE AMERICAN NEWS NETWORK. MAY THIS BE THE FIRST OF MANY NEWSCASTS WE'LL BE SHARING.
ANN
LIVE
SPECIAL REPORT

THE TIMING OF OUR FIRST BROADCAST COULDN'T BE MORE FITTING, FOR TODAY, JULY 4, 1776, WE AS A NATION FIND OURSELVES AT THE DAWN OF A NEW ERA.
IN CONGRESS, JULY 4, 1776.
The unanimous Declaration of the thirteen united States of America,

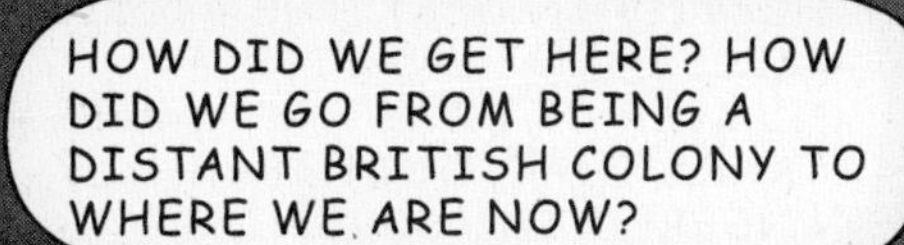

THE DECLARATION OF INDEPENDENCE:
AN ANN NEWS SPECIAL

I SUPPOSE INDEPENDENCE, AS AN IDEAL, BEGAN TO REALLY TAKE HOLD HERE AFTER THE FRENCH AND INDIAN WAR, FROM ABOUT 1763 ONWARD.
TERENCE WITHERSPOON
POLITICAL HISTORIAN
HEAVILY IN DEBT, THE BRITISH PARLIAMENT ENACTED A NUMBER OF LAWS—ACTS AND TAXES THAT, QUITE FRANKLY, ANGERED THE COLONISTS.
£
THE CURRENCY ACT, THE SUGAR ACT, THE QUARTERING ACT—ALL OF THESE LAWS MADE THE COLONISTS BELIEVE THAT THE BRITISH MONARCHY WAS OPPRESSING THEM.
SUGAR
THEN, OF COURSE, THERE WAS THE STAMP ACT.
IN 1765, THE BRITISH PARLIAMENT PASSED THE STAMP ACT, WHICH WAS SEEN AS A DIRECT TAX ON THE COLONISTS THEMSELVES!
THIS TAX WAS ONE OF MANY EVENTS THAT IGNITED THE REVOLUTION.
SO A WIDER GULF BEGAN TO DEVELOP BETWEEN BRITAIN AND THE COLONIES.

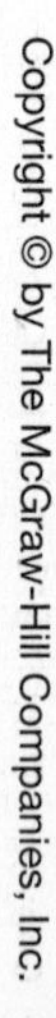

AMERICANS HAD ALREADY BEGUN TO SEE THEMSELVES AS AN INDEPENDENT, AUTONOMOUS NATION.
BRITAIN WAS SEEN AS THE OPPRESSIVE MONARCHY THAT TOOK MONEY AND JOBS FROM THE HARD-WORKING COLONISTS.
EVENTUALLY, THE STAMP ACT WAS REPEALED, BUT THE TENSION BETWEEN BRITAIN AND THE COLONISTS REMAINED.
IN 1770, THINGS REACHED A BOILING POINT WITH THE INFAMOUS "BOSTON MASSACRE." WE SPOKE TO A WITNESS OF THAT DAY'S EVENTS:
THERE WERE A NUMBER OF IDLE BRITISH SOLDIERS THERE, JUST LOAFING ABOUT. AS AMERICANS, WE WERE ALREADY ANGRY THAT THEY WERE TAKING VALUABLE JOBS.
ONE THING LED TO ANOTHER, AND WE BEGAN TO THROW SNOWBALLS AT THEM.
WILLIAM JOHNSON
BOSTON SHOPKEEPER
I'LL NEVER FORGET THE FACE OF THE FIRST MAN KILLED. HE WAS A FORMER SLAVE I THINK.
HIS NAME WAS CRISPUS ATTUCKS.
FIVE AMERICANS DIED THAT DAY. CONTINUING DISGUST WITH BRITISH RULE PEAKED AGAIN IN 1773.
THIS TIME, AS BEFORE, IT WAS IN BOSTON.
THE TEA ACT ALLOWED BRITISH EXPORTERS TO SELL CHEAPER TEA DIRECTLY TO THE COLONIES.
SINCE THIS WOULD BYPASS AMERICAN MERCHANTS, THEIR REACTION WAS PREDICTABLY ANGRY.
AT THE "BOSTON TEA PARTY," COLONISTS DESTROYED CRATES OF TEA TO EXPRESS THEIR FRUSTRATION.

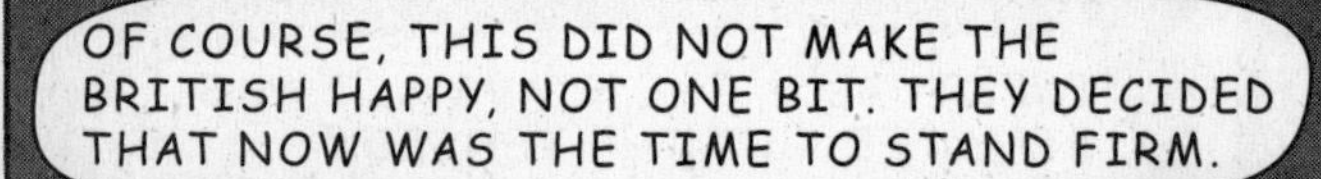

THUS, PARLIAMENT PASSED THE COERCIVE ACTS (OR INTOLERABLE ACTS AS WE AMERCANS CALLED THEM) IN 1774.

IN RESPONSE, A CONTINENTAL CONGRESS CONVENED TO DRAFT A DECLARATON OF RIGHTS AND GRIEVANCES. THIS WAS SENT TO THE KING.

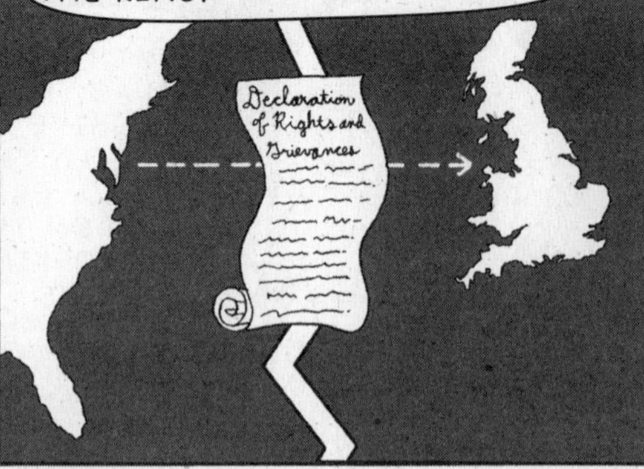

WE WERE ON THE BRINK OF WAR. AMERICANS FELT UNJUSTLY TAXED AND OPPRESSED. THE BRITISH BELIEVED THAT THEIR COLONY, THEIR PROPERTY, WAS BEING REBELLIOUS AND DEFIANT.

IN 1775, THE FIRST SHOT OF THE REVOLUTIONARY WAR WAS HEARD IN LEXINGTON, MASSACHUSETTS, NEAR CONCORD.

THIS SKIRMISH WAS THE BEGINNING OF WHAT MANY FELT WAS AN INEVITABLE WAR, A WAR WE FIGHT TO THIS VERY DAY!

MORE BATTLES WERE WAGED IN THE COMING MONTHS; THE TAKING OF FORT TICONDEROGA AND THE BATTLE OF BUNKER HILL. A SOUTHERN WAR HERO AGREED TO LEAD AMERICA'S INEXPERIENCED MILITARY FORCE: GEORGE WASHINGTON.

THE ISSUE OF INDEPENDENCE, HOWEVER, WAS STILL BEING DEBATED. SHOULD SELF-RULE BE DEMANDED, OR COULD A COMPROMISE BE FOUND?

THOMAS PAINE'S "COMMON SENSE" ARGUED STRONGLY FOR INDEPENDENCE.

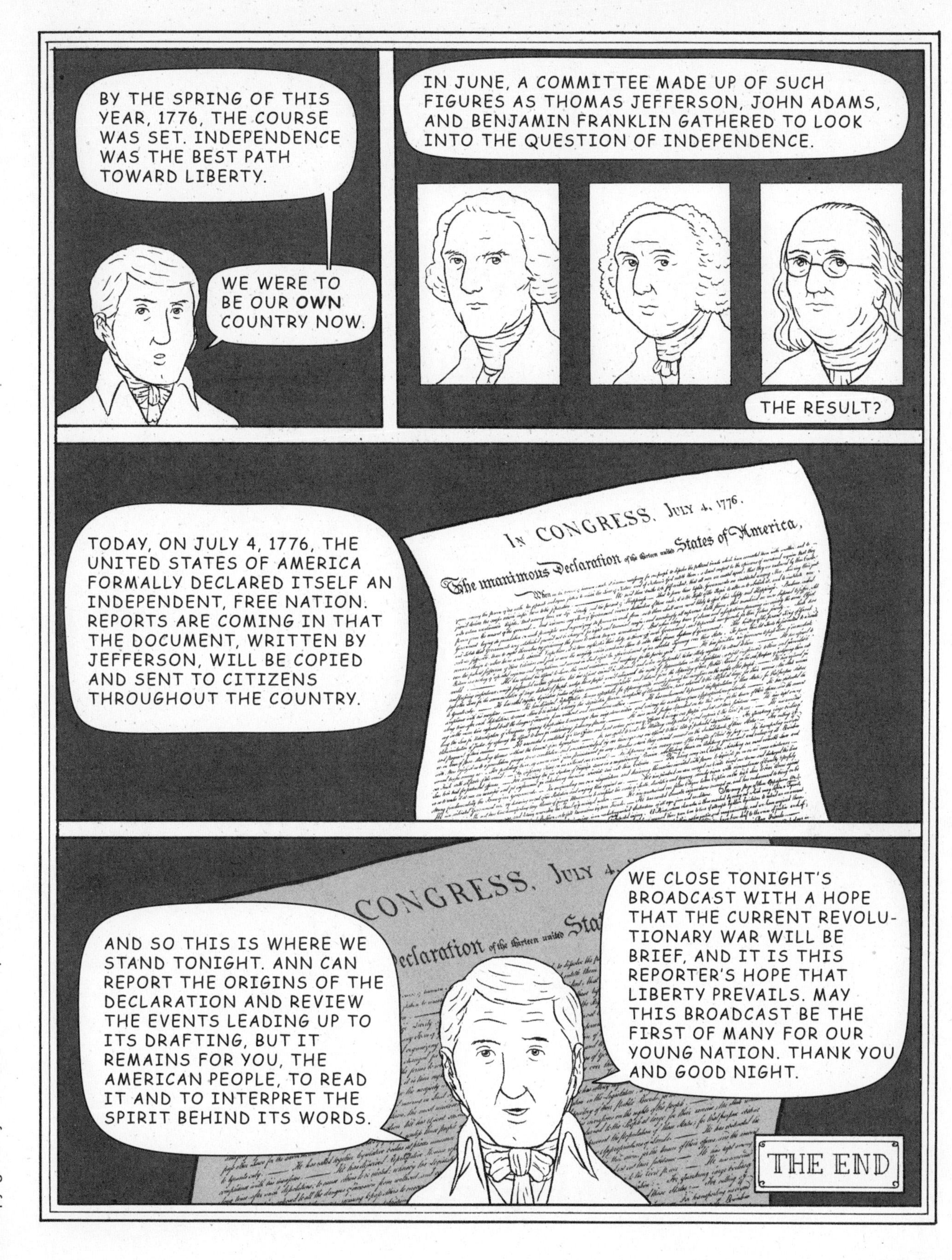
BY THE SPRING OF THIS YEAR, 1776, THE COURSE WAS SET. INDEPENDENCE WAS THE BEST PATH TOWARD LIBERTY.
WE WERE TO BE OUR **OWN** COUNTRY NOW.
IN JUNE, A COMMITTEE MADE UP OF SUCH FIGURES AS THOMAS JEFFERSON, JOHN ADAMS, AND BENJAMIN FRANKLIN GATHERED TO LOOK INTO THE QUESTION OF INDEPENDENCE.
THE RESULT?
TODAY, ON JULY 4, 1776, THE UNITED STATES OF AMERICA FORMALLY DECLARED ITSELF AN INDEPENDENT, FREE NATION. REPORTS ARE COMING IN THAT THE DOCUMENT, WRITTEN BY JEFFERSON, WILL BE COPIED AND SENT TO CITIZENS THROUGHOUT THE COUNTRY.
IN CONGRESS, JULY 4, 1776.
The unanimous Declaration of the thirteen united States of America,
AND SO THIS IS WHERE WE STAND TONIGHT. ANN CAN REPORT THE ORIGINS OF THE DECLARATION AND REVIEW THE EVENTS LEADING UP TO ITS DRAFTING, BUT IT REMAINS FOR YOU, THE AMERICAN PEOPLE, TO READ IT AND TO INTERPRET THE SPIRIT BEHIND ITS WORDS.
WE CLOSE TONIGHT'S BROADCAST WITH A HOPE THAT THE CURRENT REVOLUTIONARY WAR WILL BE BRIEF, AND IT IS THIS REPORTER'S HOPE THAT LIBERTY PREVAILS. MAY THIS BROADCAST BE THE FIRST OF MANY FOR OUR YOUNG NATION. THANK YOU AND GOOD NIGHT.
THE END

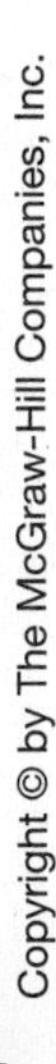

The Seneca Falls Convention
JULY 19-20, 1848
S N
STARRING:
LUCRETIA MOTT
ELIZABETH CADY STANTON
FREDERICK DOUGLASS
Leading advocate for the abolition of SLAVERY
Activist for WOMEN'S RIGHTS
Author of "Narrative of the Life of Frederick Douglass, An American SLAVE"

UPSTATE NEW YORK, 1848
Well, Elizabeth, I can't believe we're finally doing it!
A conference for women's rights - the first EVER!

And right here in Seneca Falls!
Who'd have thought it possible?

Well, we'd best get to work...
I'd like your opinion on my keynote speech. I've been really struggling.

SEVERAL HOURS LATER...
Good night, Elizabeth. It's time for you to put pen to paper and write a speech that everyone will remember!
I certainly will. You've truly inspired me, Lucretia - good night!

LATER THAT EVENING...
It's 3 A.M. - and still NOTHING!
I can't disappoint Lucretia!

What are YOU looking at?
JEFFERSON
Hmmmm.....
Thomas Jefferson... that reminds me of something!

THAT'S IT! Women in this country pay taxes but can't vote. It's just like...
TAXATION WITHOUT REPRESENTATION!
JEFFERSON

Aha! "We hold these truths to be self-evident, that all men - and WOMEN - are created EQUAL!"
Yes, that's it!

And they say the revolutionary spirit is dead!
JEFFERSON

THE NEXT WEEK
Excuse me, Elizabeth -
WHAT did you say?
"...and our right to the elective franchise."

The right to vote- for WOMEN? You'll make us utterly ridiculous - it's unprecedented!
We deserve to have some say in government - there are no two ways about it!

But it's MAD! Ask ANYONE - ask your HUSBAND -
He's one of the most progressive men I know!
All right - HENRY!!!!

What is it, ladies?
How can I be of service?
Votes for women - what do you think about THAT?

EGADS! It's...UNNATURAL!

If you persist, Elizabeth, I'm going to boycott your convention - I swear it!
Oh, swear away! I WILL find someone to second my motion at the convention...
And I have JUST the person in mind!

Message!
Message for Mr. Frederick Douglass!
THE NORTH STAR
NORTH

Votes for women?!
I'll just jot down a quick reply.

JULY 20, 1848
My, it's as packed today as it was yesterday!
I contend that the history of mankind...
...is the history of man's oppression of women!
Hear!
Hear!
I second that motion!

I deplore the fact that the nation's colleges and universities only accept MALE students!
Hear! Hear!
I second that motion!

I protest that men have control over our personal property, even the wages we earn!
Hear! Hear!
We second that motion!

And finally, I object to the fact that women have been denied the right to vote.
GASP!!

Will no one second this motion? It is the key to all our freedoms!
Certainly NOT!
She's lost her MIND!

I WILL!

Ladies and gentlemen,
the chair recognizes Mr. Frederick Douglass!
Is it really HIM?
Oh my!

Ladies and gentleman, you may know me as an advocate for the abolition of slavery, as an author, and as a newspaper publisher. I am also an escaped slave.
As a slave I knew beatings and imprisonment. You don't have to tell ME how it feels to be denied one's basic rights as a human being.
Why, I ask, do we continue to deny WOMEN their basic rights?
I hold women to be justly entitled to ALL the same rights as men.

Elizabeth Cady Stanton, I SECOND your motion to include women's right to vote as one of the liberties we demand here today.

The right to vote - for EVERY citizen!
The right to VOTE!
Hooray!
Hooray!

OHIO, 1920
Oh, I would have LOVED to have been there - Elizabeth Cady Stanton, she's my hero!
I'm writing a paper on her in my college course.
US POST OFFICE
1913

Oh, and FREDERICK DOUGLASS! If only I could go back in time and see how it all started - you know, at the SENECA FALLS CONVENTION!

That's funny, I think they'd like to be here, and see THIS...
What do you mean?

Votes for women!
It's taken YEARS, but we're finally VOTING!
BALLOT BOX
E. Lindner, 2005

WESTWARD, HO!
CALIFORNIA 2,275 mi.
With your host, Barry Bartman!
It's a 2,000-mile race across America!
Coming soon to The Frontier Network!
FTV
DISCOVERING TELEVISION

FIRST, OUR FAMILIES...JOSIAH AND NANCY CAMPBELL HAIL FROM ILLINOIS. THEIR TWO DAUGHTERS, SUSAN AND SARAH, ALONG WITH BABY BRIAN, MAKE UP THE REST OF THE TEAM.

THE WARNERS ARE FROM OHIO. ABRAHAM AND MAE HAVE THREE CHILDREN, ABE JR., FRANCES, AND ALISTAIR. BOTH FAMILIES ARE HEADED TO CALIFORNIA IN SEARCH OF GOLD.

LAST WEEK, THE WARNERS WON A MAJOR VICTORY IN THE BUFFALO ROPING COMPETITION. DAUGHTER FRANCES WAS THE HERO, LASSOING THE BUFFALO AND BRINGING IT DOWN TO WIN THE CHALLENGE!

YEE-HAW!

IT WAS ANOTHER TOUGH LOSS FOR THE CAMPBELLS, AND JOSIAH TOOK THE LOSS HARD.

...I RECKON THEY JUST HAD MORE MUSCLE'N WE DID.
WE'LL GET 'EM NEXT TIME.

SO, WE JOIN OUR FAMILIES ALONG THE TRAIL...THEY'RE NEARLY NECK AND NECK AT THIS STAGE OF THE COMPETITION, AND AWAIT TODAY'S CHALLENGE!

...I DON'T KNOW, ABE. THIS LAND IS SO NEW TO US. IT FEELS LIKE THERE'S DANGER EVERY-WHERE.
WE'LL BE ALL RIGHT, NANCY...JUST GOTTA STAY CAUTIOUS.

...HAVEN'T SEEN ANY TROUBLE YET, BUT BETTER SAFE THAN SORRY, I SUPPOSE.
BOYS!

SCOUT ON UP AHEAD A PIECE...I DON'T WANT ANYTHING TAKIN' US BY SURPRISE!
SURE, PA!

DADDY SURE DOESN'T LIKE LOSING,DOES HE?
HE'S GOT A LOT ON HIS MIND, SWEETIE.

HE'S GOT TO PUT IT PAST HIM...THE GIRLS HAVE FORGOTTEN ABOUT IT, AND SO SHOULD HE.

WHEN ARE WE GONNA STOP TO EAT, MA? MY FEET SURE ARE TIRED...
DADDY'LL TELL US WHEN WE CAN STOP.
PAW! PAW!

ABEY STEPPED ON A HORNET'S NEST!
DEY'S ALL OVER ME!

OWWWW!
GIT 'EM!
HOLD STILL, BOY!
OOOOOH, THAT'S GOTTA HURT!
NEVER A DULL MOMENT HERE ON THE GREAT PLAINS!

WELCOME TO TODAY'S CHALLENGE! THIS IS THE DIABLO RIVER...YOUR TASK IS, SIMPLY, TO CROSS IT.
BUT BEWARE... THE DEPTH IS INCONSISTENT, AND THE CURRENT IS SWIFT!

THE FIRST FAMILY TO MAKE IT ACROSS WILL NOT ONLY HAVE A HEAD START ON THIS STAGE OF THE JOURNEY, BUT WILL RECEIVE THIS CRATE OF NOURISHING OSTRICH JERKY AS A REWARD!
SO PICK YOUR SPOT...
OSTRICH JERKY

...AND
GO!

WHEN I SAW THAT RIVER I THOUGHT "NO WAY!"...

"...BUT DADDY FOUND A GOOD PLACE TO CROSS, AND WE MADE IT ACROSS RELATIVELY EASY!"

BUT THE CAMPBELLS ARE HAVING NO SUCH LUCK...
IT'S TOO DEEP! WE'LL HAVE TO GO BACK, AND TRY ANOTHER ROU-
YEOW!
JOSIAH!

I'M ALL RIGHT! HEAD FOR WHERE THE WARNERS WENT ACROSS! WE'LL GET ACROSS THERE!

PULL!
PULL!

THE CAMPBELLS HAVE FINALLY MADE IT ACROSS THE RIVER...

...BUT THEY'RE HOURS BEHIND THE WARNERS, WHO HAVE WON YET ANOTHER CHALLENGE!

WE GOTTA KEEP MOVIN', IF WE'RE GONA GET THROUGH THIS HOSTILE TERRITORY BY NIGHTFALL!

BACK IN THE CAMPBELL CAMP...
IT'S TOO LATE AND WE'VE LOST TOO MUCH TIME...
WE'LL SECURE THE WAGON AND GEAR, AND SETTLE HERE FOR THE NIGHT.
BUT JOSIAH, WHAT ABOUT THE PREDATORY ANIMALS... IS IT SAFE HERE?

NANCY, WE'VE BEEN OUT HERE FOR WEEKS, AND HOW MANY OF 'EM HAVE WE SEEN SO FAR? ZERO, THAT'S HOW MANY. I'M THINKIN' THEY'RE MORE SCARED OF US THAN WE ARE O' THEM...
AND BESIDES, I RECKON WHAT WE REALLY NEED TO CONCERN OURSELVES WITH THIS EVENIN'...

...IS THAT STORM!

JOSIAH'S DECISION PROVES TO BE A GOOD ONE, AS...
KA-BOOM

SOUNDS LIKE A DOOZY OF A STORM OUT THERE...WONDER HOW THE WARNERS ARE HOLDING UP?

TARNATION!

THE NEXT DAY...
...NEVER SHOULDA TRIED TO TRAVEL THROUGH THE NIGHT. THE STORM WASHED AWAY A BUNCH OF OUR SUPPLIES, ABOUT TOPPLED THE WAGON...

...IT'LL TAKE US DAYS TO RECOVER FROM THI-
HEY, NEIGHBOR!

SEEYA ON THE WEST COAST! YEE-HAW!
THAT'S LIFE ON THE GREAT PLAINS!
TUNE IN NEXT WEEK FOR MORE...
...WESTWARD, HO!

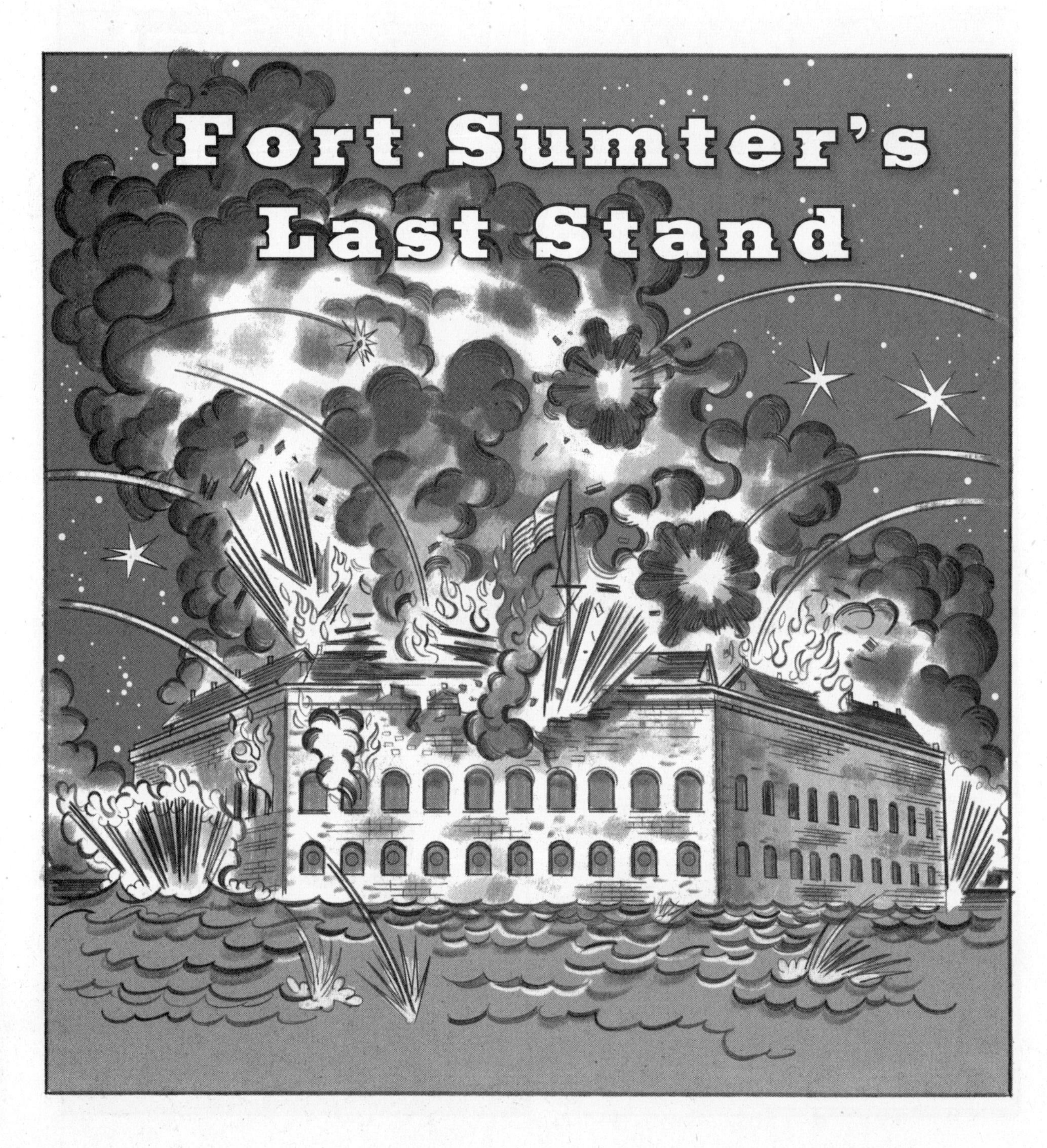
Fort Sumter's
Last Stand

FORT SUMTER, 1861

OFFICE OF CAPTAIN CHARLES TUCKER, U.S.

IT SEEMS AS THOUGH WE MAY COME IN HARM'S WAY SOONER THAN I ANTICIPATED.

THE MEN ARE ON EDGE, BUT MAJOR ANDERSON SEEMS CONFIDENT.

SIX DAYS AFTER SOUTH CAROLINA SECEDED, WE MOVED TO OUR POSITION AT FT. SUMTER.

SOUTH CAROLINA SECESSION RALLY
DEC. 20, 1860

WE MUST STAND OUR GROUND AND UPHOLD THE UNION AT ALL COST.

THERE HAS BEEN TALK OF COMPROMISE.

SEN. JOHN CRITTENDEN HAS PROPOSED THAT LINCOLN ALLOW THE SOUTH TO KEEP SLAVERY. . .

...INCLUDING ANY NEWLY FORMED SOUTHERN STATES.

THIS MUST NOT BE ALLOWED TO HAPPEN.

PRESIDENT LINCOLN'S INAUGURATION
MARCH 4, 1861

THANKFULLY OUR NEW PRESIDENT OPPOSES THIS IDEA.

WE HAVE ONLY A FEW WEEKS OF SUPPLIES LEFT.

MAJOR ANDERSON HAS REQUESTED A SUPPLY SHIP, BUT IT MAY NOT GET THROUGH.

OFFICE OF CONFEDERATE PRESIDENT JEFFERSON DAVIS

THIS MUST BE STOPPED!

TO: GEN. P.G.T BEAUREGARD
FROM: PRES. JEFFERSON DAVIS
REMOVE UNION PRESENCE IN CHARLESTON HARBOR AT ALL COST.

FORT SUMTER: APRIL 12, 1861

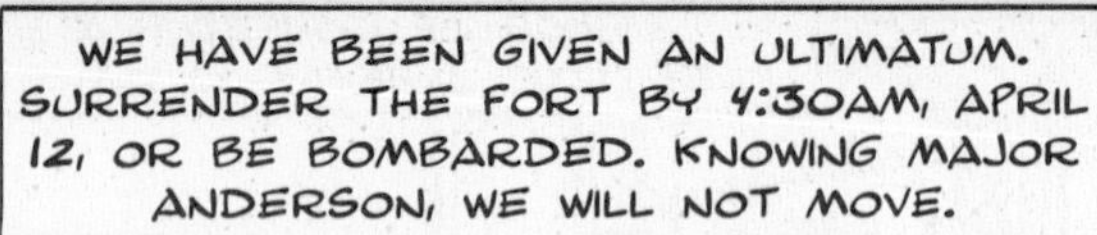
WE HAVE BEEN GIVEN AN ULTIMATUM. SURRENDER THE FORT BY 4:30AM, APRIL 12, OR BE BOMBARDED. KNOWING MAJOR ANDERSON, WE WILL NOT MOVE.

MAJOR ROBERT ANDERSON
GENTLEMEN, THE HOUR IS UPON US.

TRY NOT TO WORRY. LOVE, CHARLES

THEME 6

MARCUS,
SARAH,
OK EVERYONE, SETTLE DOWN, I HAVE A FUN CLASS PREPARED TODAY. DREW, WOULD YOU MIND TURNING OFF THE LIGHTS?
READ!
GREAT, LET'S GET STARTED.
TODAY WE'RE GOING TO TALK ABOUT THE IMPORTANCE OF THE...
BUFFALO
OH, THAT REMINDS ME, TODAY THE CAFETERIA IS SERVING BUFFALO WINGS!
CARL BRINGS UP A VALID QUESTION...
WHAT IF THE CAFETERIA RAN OUT OF THOSE BUFFALO WINGS?
I'D PROBABLY JUST EAT SOME OF THE POTATO CHIPS I HAVE HIDDEN IN MY LOCKER.
WELL, THE NATIVE AMERICANS OF THE GREAT PLAINS DIDN'T HAVE THAT OPTION...

THE BUFFALO, ALSO KNOWN AS THE AMERICAN BISON, WAS ESSENTIAL FOR THE SURVIVAL OF THE NATIVE AMERICANS OF THE WEST.
BUFFALO PROVIDED NOT ONLY FOOD, BUT ALSO MATERIALS FOR SHELTER AND CLOTHES.
BONES WERE USED FOR TOOL MAKING, DECORATION, ARTWORK, TOYS, AND GAMES.
CAN YOU THINK OF ONE ITEM THAT YOU UTILIZE IN EVERY ASPECT OF YOUR LIFE?
MY LAPTOP?
CELL-PHONES?
TV!
CARS!
SURE, THOSE THINGS MAKE LIFE EASIER, BUT YOU COULD GET BY WITHOUT THEM IF YOU HAD TO!
I DON'T THINK I COULD SURVIVE IF I COULDN'T WATCH "WESTWARD HO!"

THE NATIVE AMERICANS USED EVERY BIT OF THE BUFFALO. THE HIDES WERE USED FOR MOCCASINS AND CLOTHING.
THREAD WAS MADE OF THE SINEWS OF THE ANIMAL MUSCLE. COOL, HUH?
THE NECK PELTS BECAME SHIELDS, AND RIBS WERE TIED TOGETHER FOR SLEDS.
EWW, GROSS!
STILL FEEL LIKE EATING THOSE BUFFALO WINGS, CARL?
BUFFALO WINGS ARE MADE FROM A CHICKEN...
THE NATIVE AMERICANS BELIEVED ELABORATE RITUALS WOULD ENSURE THAT THE BUFFALO WOULD REMAIN PLENTIFUL. THESE DANCES WERE PASSED FROM ONE GENERATION TO THE NEXT.
THAT LOOKS LIKE A CRAZY DANCE PARTY!
ACTUALLY, IT'S VERY CAREFULLY CHOREO-GRAPHED.
COOL!

SADLY, BY THE END OF THE 19TH CENTURY AS FEW AS 750 BUFFALO REMAINED. HUNTING IS PARTLY TO BLAME.
HOWEVER THE NEW RAILROAD COMPANIES ALSO PAID TO DESTROY ENTIRE HERDS BECAUSE BUFFALO ON THE TRACKS COULD DAMAGE AN ONCOMING LOCOMOTIVE.
AS THE HERDS DWINDLED IN NUMBER, THE NATIVE AMERICANS TRIED TO MAINTAIN THEIR WAY OF LIFE.
EVENTUALLY, HOWEVER, THEY HAD TO MAKE THE DECISION TO CHANGE THEIR WAY OF LIFE AND BEGAN TO SETTLE ON U.S. GOVERNMENT RESERVATIONS.
THAT MUST HAVE BEEN, LIKE, REALLY HARD.
CAN YOU IMAGINE LOSING SOMETHING SO IMPORTANT AND TRYING TO REBUILD YOUR LIFE AFTER IT'S GONE?
MY AUNT LOST HER HOUSE IN A BIG HURRICANE ONCE.
YEAH, BUT IT'S NOT LIKE HER WHOLE WAY OF LIFE CHANGED.

TODAY, THANKS TO HELP FROM ACROSS THE ENTIRE COUNTRY, THE AMERICAN BUFFALO POPULATION HAS GROWN TO ABOUT 350,000.

THIS MAY SEEM LIKE A LOT, BUT NOT IN COMPARISON TO THE ESTIMATED 100 MILLION THAT EXISTED IN THE 17TH AND 18TH CENTURIES.

BUZZZ!
ALRIGHT EVERYONE, WE'll CONTINUE THIS DISCUSSION NEXT TIME. THAT'S LUNCH, CLASS DISMISSED!

CAN I BRING A BUFFALO NICKEL IN FOR EXTRA CREDIT?
MAN, ALL THAT TALK ABOUT BUFFALO MADE ME EVEN MORE HUNGRY FOR THOSE SPICY BUFFALO WINGS!
I THOUGHT YOU SAID THAT THEY'RE FROM A CHICKEN!
HOMEWORK
BY BRIAN RALPH
THE END!

Jeannette Rankin

First Woman in Congress

IN 1916, JEANNETTE PICKERING RANKIN BECAME THE FIRST WOMAN ELECTED TO THE UNITED STATES CONGRESS, FOUR YEARS BEFORE ALL WOMEN IN THE UNITED STATES HAD THE RIGHT TO VOTE.

SHE ARRIVED IN WASHINGTON WHEN EVERYONE WAS TALKING ABOUT DECLARING WAR ON GERMANY.

RANKIN FACED ONE OF THE MOST DIFFICULT DECISIONS OF HER LIFE. SHE THOUGHT BACK TO ALL HER STRUGGLES CAMPAIGNING FOR WOMAN SUFFRAGE.

SHE WAS THE FIRST WOMAN TO APPROACH THE MONTANA STATE LEGISLATURE TO SUBMIT THE WOMAN SUFFRAGE BILL.

JEANNETTE GAVE HER ROUSING AND ELOQUENT SPEECH TO A PACKED HOUSE OF THE MONTANA STATE LEGISLATURE ON FEBRUARY 11, 1911.

IN 1913, THE NATIONAL AMERICAN WOMAN SUFFRAGE ASSOCIATION (NAWSA) ORGANIZED A PARADE AND MARCH IN WASHINGTON, D.C., TO INCREASE NATIONAL ATTENTION. ON MARCH 3, 1913, RANKIN JOINED 5,000 OTHERS IN THE MARCH ON PENNSYLVANIA AVENUE.

THE POLICE UNDERESTIMATED THE FORCE NEEDED FOR CROWD CONTROL, AND THE MARCH TURNED INTO A RIOT. WOMEN WERE TAUNTED AND SPAT UPON. SEVERAL HUNDRED WOMEN WERE INJURED.

WITH SUFFRAGE NOW A BLAZING HOT ISSUE ACROSS THE COUNTRY, RANKIN RETURNED TO MONTANA, WHERE SHE LED THE SUFFRAGE CAMPAIGN TO A STATEWIDE VICTORY IN 1914.

IN 1916, JEANNETTE RAN FOR A SEAT IN THE U.S. HOUSE OF REPRESENTATIVES. HER PLATFORM CONSISTED OF SUFFRAGE FOR WOMEN, INFANT AND MATERNAL HEALTH CARE, AN EIGHT-HOUR WORKDAY FOR WOMEN, TAX LAW REFORM, AND PEACE.

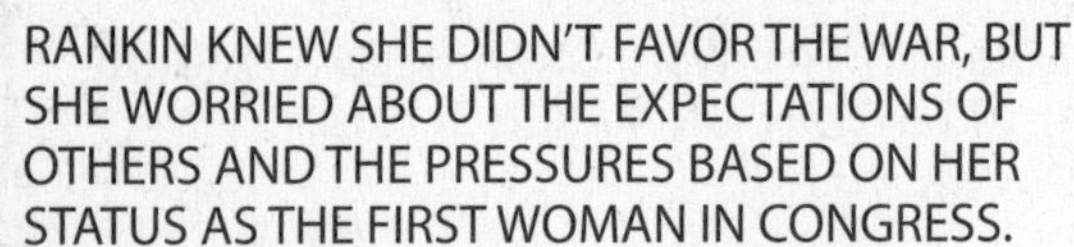

THE NAWSA PRESIDENT, CARRIE CHAPMAN CATT, BELIEVED THAT WOMEN WOULD BE SEEN AS WEAK AND IMPRACTICAL IF RANKIN SHOULD VOTE AGAINST WAR.

HER CLOSE FRIENDS AND FAMILY, INCLUDING HER BROTHER AND CAMPAIGN MANAGER WELLINGTON, URGED HER TO VOTE FOR WAR.

IN THE END, JEANNETTE RANKIN ALWAYS VOTED WITH HER CONSCIENCE.

WE'RE OFF TO SEE THE PRES!
Gregory Benton

I GUESS WE CAN STOP FOR TODAY.

DON'T QUITE KNOW WHY WE WORK SO DARNED HARD, MAMA.

OUR CROPS SELL FOR PRACTICALLY *NOTHING*.
WE DON'T MAKE ENOUGH TO PAY THE BANK *OR* GET SUPPLIES.
AND THERE'S NO DEMAND...

IT'S JUST GONNA ROT!
MAYBE PRESIDENT ROOSEVELT CAN HELP, DADDY!

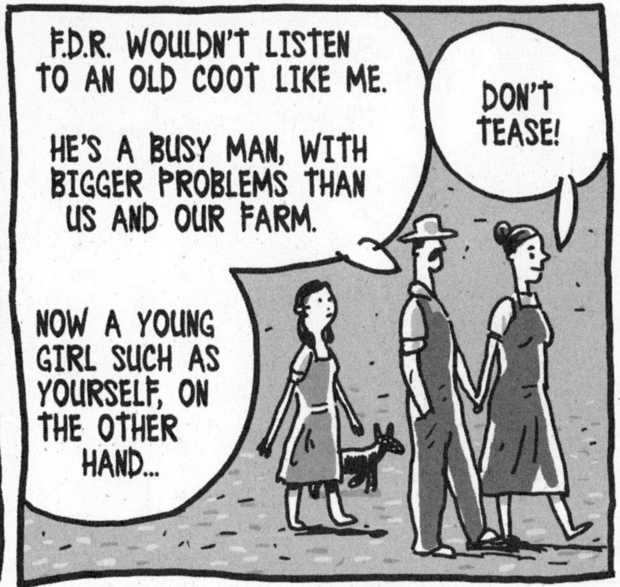
F.D.R. WOULDN'T LISTEN TO AN OLD COOT LIKE ME.
HE'S A BUSY MAN, WITH BIGGER PROBLEMS THAN US AND OUR FARM.
DON'T TEASE!
NOW A YOUNG GIRL SUCH AS YOURSELF, ON THE OTHER HAND...

LATER THAT NIGHT...
MOM, WHERE IS WASHINGTON, D.C.?
OH, DEAR... BACK EAST, WHERE THE SUN RISES.

SWEET DREAMS.
G'NIGHT!

I THINK SHE'S WORRIED BY WHAT YOU SAID THIS AFTERNOON...
SHE'LL GET OVER IT COME MORNING.
KANSAS TRIBUNE

Dear mom. gone to D.C.

I'LL NEVER GET THERE IF I RUN ALL THE WAY...

HEY, WHAT'S GOING ON HERE?
THIS IS A SOUP LINE.

WE ALL LOST OUR JOBS, SO WE WAIT IN LINE FOR FREE FOOD.

BUT THAT'S NOT UNUSUAL. ALL ACROSS THE COUNTRY...

PEOPLE

NEED

HELP!
apples 1¢
PENCILS 1¢

I GUESS MY DAD IS NOT THE ONLY ONE!
FAIR WAGE!
HELP!
JOBS

HELLO, BIRDS!
I'VE BEEN FLYING ALL
NIGHT! IS WASHINGTON, D.C. NEAR?

JUST BELOW
YOU!

THANK YOU!

LOOK OUT
BELOW!

EXCUSE ME,
WHERE CAN I
FIND
F.D.R.?
OVER THERE.
BUT YOU
CAN'T GET
IN.
WE'VE BEEN TRYING
FOR DAYS.
I HEARD HE'S
SCARY!

EXCUSE ME, SIR.
WE'VE COME A LONG WAY
TO SPEAK WITH F.D.R.
MAY WE GO IN,
PLEASE?
O.K.

MAY I HELP
YOU?

MY FRIENDS
AND I WOULD
LIKE A MOMENT
WITH THE GREAT
AND POWERFUL...

F.D.R.

MR. PRESIDENT? YOU HAVE SOME VISITORS...

GO ON IN. HE'S BEEN EXPECTING YOU.

GOSH!!

WELCOME! I'M PLEASED TO SEE YOU ALL!

HOW CAN I BE OF SERVICE?
AFTER ALL, I WORK FOR YOU!

WE ALL HAVE SOME QUESTIONS.
GO ON.

IS THERE ANYTHING YOU CAN DO FOR THE WORKING CLASS?
ANYTHING THAT COULD PROVIDE A LIVING WAGE?

MY CONSTRUCTION BUSINESS HAS GROUND TO A HALT.
CAN YOU PUT US TO WORK? WE'LL BUILD ANYTHING!

CAN YOU HELP RESTORE THE CONFIDENCE OF THE AMERICAN PEOPLE?
WE'RE TIRED OF BEING SCARED!

I JUST WANT MY FATHER TO BE HAPPY.
OUR FARM ISN'T DOING TOO WELL.

YOU'VE CERTAINLY VISITED AT THE RIGHT TIME... I HAVE ANSWERS FOR YOU ALL!

WE'RE GOING TO GIVE WIDESPREAD EMPLOYMENT THROUGH THE CIVILIAN CONSERVATION CORPS!

AND THE PUBLIC WORKS ADMINISTRATION WILL PUT COMPANIES TO WORK BUILDING BRIDGES, ROADS, AND BUILDINGS!

THIS WILL ALL BE UNDER THE UMBRELLA OF THE NEW DEAL. I BELIEVE IT WILL MAKE AMERICA FEEL BETTER ABOUT ITSELF!

AS FOR AGRICULTURE: WE'LL HELP THE FARMERS GET THEIR PRODUCE TO THE MARKET.
TELL YOUR DAD NOT TO WORRY WHEN YOU WAKE UP!

WAKE UP?!
OH!

DADDY! DADDY!!

PRESIDENT ROOSEVELT SAID FOR YOU NOT TO WORRY!
I KNOW! YOUR MOTHER AND I WERE JUST LISTENING TO HIM ON THE RADIO!
YOU WERE RIGHT...
F.D.R. CARED AND HELPED!
end

THEME 9

OKAY, DEAR. JUST MAKE SURE YOU'RE HERE TO DEAL WITH THAT SALESMAN.
BECAUSE I THINK THE WHOLE SUBJECT IS DREADFUL! I DON'T WANT TO THINK ABOUT IT!
SEE YOU AT 5 O'CLOCK, SWEETIE.
KNOCK-KNOCK!
OH MY, NOW WHO COULD THAT BE?
HELLO?
56
GOOD AFTERNOON. MRS. WHITTEN, ISN'T IT? I REPRESENT WISHING WELL CONSTRUCTION.
MY NAME'S VICTOR RAND.

I HOPE YOU DON'T MIND THAT I'M SO EARLY FOR OUR APPOINTMENT.
I DON'T SUPPOSE THIS MEANS MR. WHITTEN IS STILL AT WORK? HE IS? TERRIBLE PITY, THAT.
BUT YOU LOOK LIKE A BRIGHT GAL. AND THE INFORMATION I HAVE SIMPLY CAN'T WAIT! MY, WHAT A LOVELY HOME YOU HAVE HERE.
CLEAN, TASTEFUL, SAFE AND EFFICIENT. EVERYTHING THAT AN AMERICAN HOME SHOULD BE.
OH, MY HUSBAND REALLY...

YES, YOU'RE A FINE HOMEMAKER, I CAN SEE THAT, WHY IT'S PLAIN AS DAY: A WOMAN WHO CARES FOR HER HUSBAND AND CHILDREN...
A WOMAN WHO KNOWS THAT IT IS HER PATRIOTIC DUTY TO KEEP HER FAMILY SAFE AND HAPPY...
BECAUSE, AFTER ALL, ISN'T FAMILY THE VERY LYNCHPIN OF OUR GREAT DEMOCRATIC SOCIETY?

OH, THAN-
BUT LET ME ASK YOU THIS- AS ONE CONCERNED CITIZEN TO ANOTHER - IS YOUR FAMILY REALLY SAFE? ARE YOU PREPARED FOR ATOMIC WAR? WHAT WOULD YOU DO IF THE COMMIES DROPPED THE BOMB AT 10:00 AM TOMORROW MORNING? WHAT WOULD YOU DO IF THEY WERE DROPPING ONE RIGHT NOW?!

OH, MY GOOD-NESS!
BECAUSE THEY COULD, YOU KNOW.
D'YOU THINK THE RUSSIANS CARE IF IT'S A THURSDAY? HAH! THEY DON'T EVEN HAVE THURS-DAYS IN RUSSIA!
EVERYDAY IS STALINDAY, AND STALINDAY IS A GOOD DAY FOR WAR, FOR ALL THEY CARE!

THINK THE *RUSSIANS* CARE THAT YOU HAVE THIS SWELL ROAST IN THE OVEN, OR THAT LITTLE SUZY'S *DANCE RECITAL* IS THIS WEEKEND?
FIDDLESTICKS!
THE *RED HORDE* DOESN'T TAKE DANCE RECITALS INTO ACCOUNT WHEN PLANNING THEIR *FIENDISH AGGRESSIONS!*

YOU'VE SEEN THE NEWSREELS! YOU KNOW ALL ABOUT THE TERRIBLE DESTRUCTIVE POWER OF THE ATOM BOMB! THE MUSHROOM CLOUD!
THE *BLAST* OF SEARING LIGHT!
THE *CRUSHING* SHOCKWAVES!
THE DEVASTATING *FIREBALL!*

THE MAELSTROM OF NUCLEAR FURY, UNLEASHED!

EEP!
"OH, BUT MR. RAND!," YOU SAY...
"WE LIVE TOO FAR FROM THE CITY. THE BOMB BLASTS WON'T REACH OUT HERE!"

BUT WHAT ABOUT THE *INVISIBLE* KILLER...
RADIATION!
RA-?
WHAT ABOUT *FALLOUT? HUH?* DID YOU THINK OF THAT?

Y'SEE, A MUSHROOM CLOUD THROWS TONS AND TONS OF DIRT AND ASH INTO THE AIR. AND THAT STUFF SPREADS *OUT,* AND *FALLS* ALL OVER THE PLACE.
THAT'S WHY WE CALL IT *"FALLOUT."*
AND WHEREVER IT FALLS IS *CONTAMINATED!*

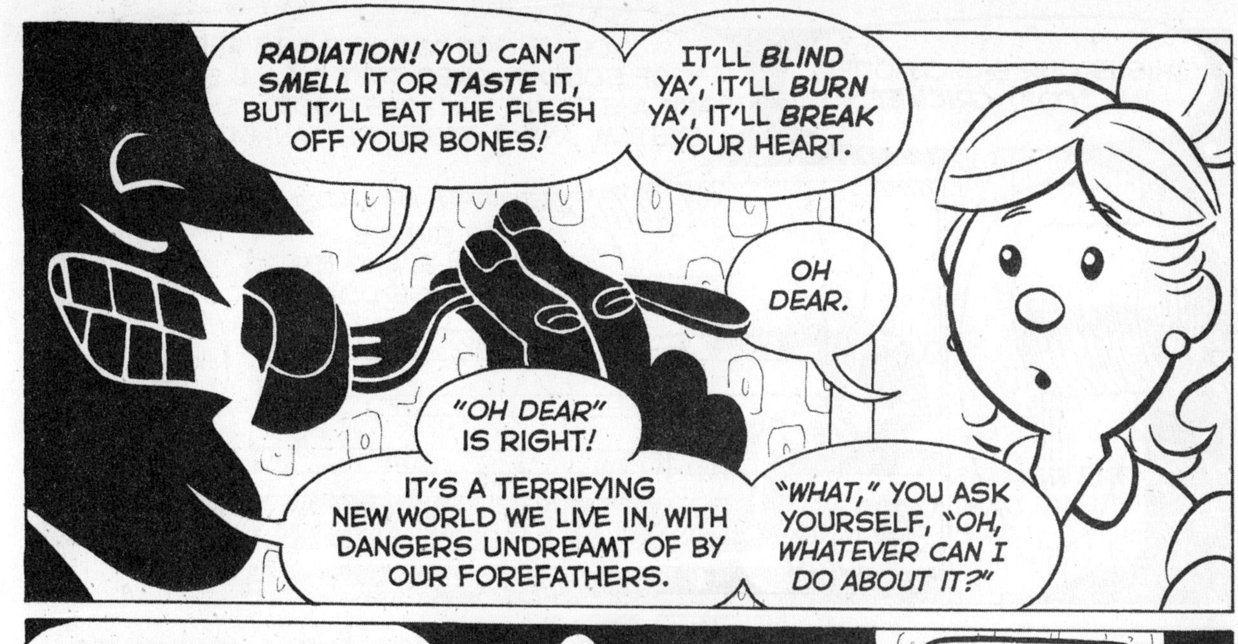
RADIATION! YOU CAN'T SMELL IT OR TASTE IT, BUT IT'LL EAT THE FLESH OFF YOUR BONES!
IT'LL BLIND YA', IT'LL BURN YA', IT'LL BREAK YOUR HEART.
OH DEAR.
"OH DEAR" IS RIGHT!
IT'S A TERRIFYING NEW WORLD WE LIVE IN, WITH DANGERS UNDREAMT OF BY OUR FOREFATHERS.
"WHAT," YOU ASK YOURSELF, "OH, WHATEVER CAN I DO ABOUT IT?"

DID YOU THINK AMERICAN INGENUITY WOULD LET YOU DOWN?
DON'T BE SILLY! YOU CAN KEEP YOUR FAMILY SAFE AND COMFY THROUGH THE WORST THOSE SAVAGE SOVIETS HAVE TO THROW AT US.
ALL IT TAKES IS A LITTLE PLANNING... AND A REASONABLE INVESTMENT IN SENSIBLE PRECAUTIONS.

THIS IS WHERE YOUR FINE FRIENDS AT WISHING WELL CONSTRUCTION COME IN.
DOWN OUR WELL
WE OFFER THE FINEST RANGE OF FALLOUT SHELTERS AVAILABLE IN THIS GREAT COUNTRY OF OURS! IT'S ALL IN OUR FREE BROCHURE.

SEE, A FALLOUT SHELTER IS A SAFE ROOM UNDERGROUND WHERE YOUR FAMILY CAN WAIT OUT ANY TROUBLE-SOME SIDE-EFFECTS OF AN ATOMIC WAR.

THIS IS OUR BASIC MODEL, THE "COZY CRICKET."
YOU'VE GOT ABOUT THREE FEET OF SOLID-PACKED DIRT ON ALL SIDES, AND A STRONG LOCKING DOOR, VENTILATION SYSTEM, AND A STORE OF CANNED FOODS.
IT'S SIMPLE, AFFORDABLE, AND IT'LL GET THE JOB DONE.
BUT THIS ROOM COULD BE YOUR HOME FOR DAYS, EVEN WEEKS. A HOMEMAKER LIKE YOURSELF KNOWS LIFE IS ABOUT MORE THAN JUST SURVIVAL! THERE'S ENJOYMENT, TOO! AND WHEN IT COMES TO BEING COOPED UP WITH YOUR FAMILY, THAT MEANS ELBOW ROOM!
WE CALL THIS THE "DELUXE GROTTO SUITE."
NOTICE THE EXPANDED ENTERTAINMENT AREA, FOR WHEN THE KIDS GET RESTLESS.
GOV'T GRADE CHEESE
AND HERE'S A COMPLETE KITCHENETTE, WHERE YOU CAN PREPARE FINE MEALS FROM FOODS GOVERNMENT-TESTED TO STAND UP TO FALLOUT CONDITIONS!
PILLS, OXYGEN
LEAD-LINED WALLS, ELECTRICAL GENERATOR, WATER SUPPLY, OXYGEN PILLS, RADIO, MURPHY BEDS, AN ESSENTIAL LIBRARY OF SURVIVAL BOOKS...

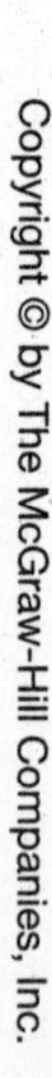

AND CHECK OUT THIS DANDY FEATURE:
PREVENT "CABIN FEVER" WITH OUR FAUX WINDOWS. AVAILABLE IN A VARIETY OF PASTORAL LANDSCAPES!
I LIKE THIS ONE, "HAWAIIAN SUNSET."
HOW LOV-
OF COURSE, NOT EVERYONE WILL BE PRUDENT ENOUGH TO BUY A SHELTER. TO PROTECT YOUR FAMILY'S PRECIOUS SURVIVAL RESOURCES WE OFFER A RANGE OF SECURITY MEASURES...
VAULT DOORS, PERIMETER MINES, SPRING-LOADED NETS, & THAT TRUSTY OL' STANDBY, THE BENGAL TIGER PIT.
WAIT IT ALL OUT IN LUXURY AND STYLE! TO DO ANY LESS WOULD BE TO LET THE COMMIES WIN!
PEAS
YES, PEACE OF MIND IN THE ATOMIC AGE IS YOURS!
ALL YOU HAVE TO DO IS SIGN HERE ON THE DOTTED LINE!
OH, MR. RAND, THAT SOUNDS WONDERFUL...
SHOULDN'T I WAIT UNTIL MY MY HUSBAND...
MR. WHITTEN WOULDN'T DARE DELAY A MOMENT ON A DECISION THIS IMPORTANT!
CONTRA
NOT WITH HIS FAMILY'S VERY FUTURE AT STAKE!
DO YOU REALLY THINK SO, MR. RAND?
THERE'S A SIGHT THAT ALWAYS MAKES MY HEART SWELL WITH RED, WHITE, AND BLUE!

THEME 10

P.S.- mom Sent me
THAT PICTURE
OF US. forgot
Like WITH HAIR!
IT your WAY So
Can HAVE A LOOK.
TAKE CARE,
THE LOTTERY

BETWEEN 1969 AND 1972, FOUR NATIONAL LOTTERIES WERE HELD TO DETERMINE THE ORDER OF CALLS FOR INDUCTION INTO THE ARMED FORCES.
MEN WITH HIGH LOTTERY NUMBERS WERE LESS LIKELY TO BE DRAFTED.

MEN WHOSE LOTTERY NUMBERS WERE LOWER WERE ALMOST CERTAIN TO BE DRAFTED AND SENT TO THE WAR IN VIETNAM.

STUDENT REGI
STUDENTS WERE GIVEN A *DEFERMENT* FROM MILTARY SERVICE.

SUPPLY

WITH AN A AVERAGE, BUT
LL MAKE IT UP NEXT QUARTER
NYWAY, HAVE YOU BEEN IN
COMBAT?
IF YOU GUYS EVER
Y LOW AND
OUT OF TROUBLE
OT TO WORRY TOO
NYWAY, YOU'RE GOING
TO MAKE IT HOME!
WRITE WHEN YOU CAN
TALK SOON
THE SOLDIERS IN VIETNAM FACED FIERCE BATTLES IN UNFAMILIAR TERRITORY.
THINGS
SCARY BUT
GO NOW.
WRITE SO
P.S.- MOM SENT ME
THAT PICTURE SHE TOOK
OF US. FORGOT WHAT I LO
LIKE WITH HAIR! I'M SE
IT YOUR WAY SO YOU CA
HAVE A LOOK.
TAKE CARE-
7-12-'70

NEARLY 60,000 SOLDIERS NEVER CAME HOME FROM VIETNAM.

THEME 11

MAY DAY

Do you ladies take any cream or sugar in your coffee?
Just a splash of milk please...
No thank you, Claire.

...Well I think what those "people" are doing is horrible. The young men of this country are in harm's way. They need our support.

I agree, Anne. This protesting is just moral support to the enemy. How does it look to our soliders risking their lives?

Well, I agree with both of you, but I don't think it's so cut and dried. These kids are not wrong for speaking out. They're concerned about people dying.
Now that the president has announced this business in Cambodia, it's even more likely that their friends and neighbors will be drafted.

MAY
1970
trash bags!!
-Milk
Tsch, Barb, don't give in to this Communist propaganda. That's what I think these people are..

...Communist sympathizers and threats to the United States.
That's right, they should all be locked up.

I don't pretend to know people's intentions. I do understand the fear of being sent of to a distant jungle to fight for your life in a war you don't understand.

My son Henry is too young right now, but I'm scared to death of the idea of him being drafted. I know you wouldn't want that for your son, Claire.

No, of course not. What mother would? Thank heavens he's away at school.
Hopefully this whole mess will be over when he graduates. At least he is safe right now.

Where does he go?
Kent State, in Ohio.

RING
Oh, that's probably him now! He calls every day to talk about how school is going. He's such a good boy.

We interupt this regularly scheduled broadcast for a special news bulletin...
UNIVERSITY SHOOTINGS
SPECIAL REPORT
Hello?

THEME 12

AND THE FINAL RESULTS FOR THE 2000 PRESEDENTIAL ELECTION ARE IN. THE WINNER IS...
AL GORE! NO, WAIT A MINUTE...
GEORGE BUSH! NO, HOLD ON. CORRECTION. OH, THE ACTUAL WINNER IS... OH, I DON'T KNOW.
I CAN'T BELIEVE THAT WE STILL DON'T KNOW WHO WON THE ELECTION!
YES, IT MUST HAVE BEEN A MIGHTY CLOSE VOTE.
NEWS
WHO IS THE WINNER?
The very close vote totals in Florida was the cause of most of the delay.
THE RESULTS HAVE TO BE VERIFIED BY THE FLORIDA GOVERNMENT.
SO WHAT THE HECK ARE WE GOING TO DO NEXT?
I THINK THAT'S CORRECT. THE FINAL CALL WILL HAVE TO COME FROM THE FLORIDA SUPREME COURT.

At the Florida Supreme Court...
WE BELIEVE THAT THE RESULTS ARE TOO CLOSE TO CALL. THEREFORE WE ORDER A RECOUNT.
MAN! THAT MUST HAVE REALLY BEEN A CLOSE CALL! I DON'T ENVY THOSE HAVING TO RECOUNT!
OH WELL... I DIDN'T HAVE PLANS FOR THE WEEKEND ANYWAY!
...1245, 1246, 1247...
...I COULD REALLY DO WITH PIZZA RIGHT NOW...
WHOSE TURN IS IT FOR THE COFFEE RUN?
HOW CLOSE DO YOU THINK THE LAST VOTE WAS?
JUST REMEMBER THAT EVERY VOTE COUNTS. YOU NEVER KNOW, IT COULD COME DOWN TO JUST ONE VOTE!
BUSH 15
GORE 14

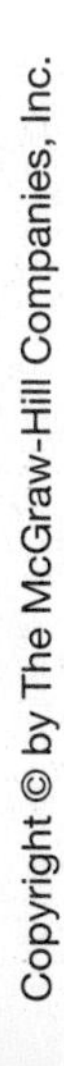

HEY GUYS! COME AND CHECK THIS OUT!
IS IT A 'BAD CHAD'?
WOW, THAT'S A NEW THING. WHAT DO YOU CALL SOMETHING LIKE THAT?
I THINK IT'S MORE OF A 'DANGLING CHAD' TO ME.
I'M NOT SURE. WE COULD CALL IT A 'SHOULD I STAY OR SHOULD I GO CHAD'.
I KINDA THINK IT'S MORE LIKE A 'LOOSE CHAD'.
I DON'T KNOW GUYS. FROM WHERE I'M STANDING, I DON'T THINK WE CAN CALL THIS ANYTHING OTHER THAN...
WELL, WE NEED TO GIVE IT SOME KIND OF NAME.
...A 'HANGING CHAD!'

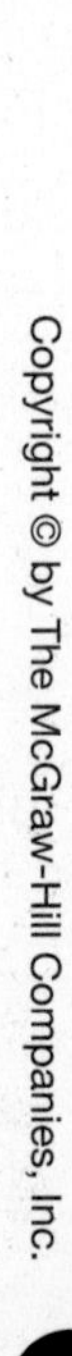

HANGING CHAD? YEAH, THAT WORKS. ANYWAY, LET'S GET BACK TO WORK. WE HAVE A LOT TO DO.
The Pizza Guy arrives...
SPEEDY PIZZA! I GOT A LARGE CHICKEN AND PINEAPPLE, HOLD THE ONIONS, HEAVY ON THE CHILI. WHO WANTS IT?
OH YES! AM I READY FOR THIS!
SNEEEEEZE!
WHO WANTS A SLICE?
WE'VE PROBABLY GOT ANOTHER TWO HOURS TO GO AND WE'LL BE FINISHED. KEEP IT UP, GUYS!

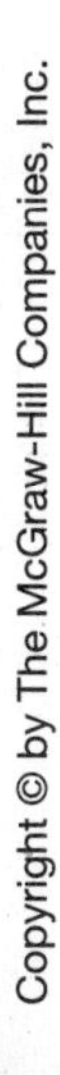

The Hanging Chad has left the building...
Outside the Florida election office building, crowds are gathering to await the results...
Bush 2
Gore 0
THIS IS GETTING REALLY EXCITING NOW!
COME ON!
BUSH IS BEST
WE WANT BUSH! WE WANT BUSH! WE WANT BUSH!
GORE
BUSH! BUSH! BUSH!
GORE IS THE ONE!
BUSH
COME ON, AL! YOU CAN DO IT!
GORE IS GOING TO DO IT! BRING IT HOME, AL!

The Hanging Chad makes its way towards the U.S. Supreme Court in Washington, D.C.
The results are due any minute...
NEWS
" NONE ARE MORE CONSCIOUS OF THE VITAL LIMITS ON JUDICIAL AUTHORITY THAN ARE THE MEMBERS OF THIS COURT, AND NONE STAND MORE IN ADMIRATION OF THE CONSTITUTION'S DESIGN TO LEAVE THE SELECTION OF THE PRESIDENT TO THE PEOPLE, THROUGH THEIR LEGISLATURES, AND TO THE POLITICAL SPHERE. WHEN CONTENDING PARTIES INVOKE THE PROCESS OF THE COURTS, HOWEVER, IT BECOMES OUR UNSOUGHT RESPONSIBILITY TO RESOLVE THE FEDERAL AND CONSTITUTIONAL ISSUES THE JUDICIAL SYSTEM HAS BEEN FORCED TO CONFRONT."

THEME 13

HARVARD UNIVERSITY, THE 1970s. THE BEST AND BRIGHTEST STUDENTS COME HERE TO RECEIVE THEIR EDUCATION. BUSINESS, LAW, POLITICS, TECHNOLOGY-- THE YOUNG PEOPLE HERE TODAY WILL GO ON TO SHAPE THE FUTURE OF THE WORLD.
OOF!

I'M OKAY! I'M OKAY!
IF ANYONE CARES, I'M OKAY!

SIGH...
NO ONE CARES...

MEANWHILE...
THERE! IT TOOK TWO SOLID WEEKS OF WORK, A HUNDRED SHEETS OF PAPER, AND THREE BOTTLES OF CORRECTION FLUID...
...BUT MY TERM PAPER IS FINALLY DONE!

TIME FOR A QUICK BREAK BEFORE THE BIG FRISBEE TOURNAMENT!
KSSHT!
SODA

WHOOPS!
FIZZZZ
SODA
SPLOOSH

OKAY, DON'T PANIC. MAYBE IT'LL DRY OUT IF I PUT THE PAGES BY THE WINDOW.

OH NO.

OH NO!

PAPER FALLING FROM THE SKY? A MOST UNUSUAL PHENOMENON.

SPEAKING OF UNUSUAL PHENOMENA...ARE YOU CRYING?
RUINED! MY PAPER IS RUINED!

WHAT SEEMS TO BE THE TROUBLE, CHUM?
I...I CAN'T BELIEVE IT!

I'VE GOT TO RETYPE THE WHOLE THING IN JUST FIVE HOURS, WHICH MEANS I HAVE TO MISS THE ULTIMATE FRISBEE TOURNAMENT!

SAY...I'VE GOT AN IDEA!
FORGET IT!

I'M NOT GOING TO RETYPE YOUR PAPER FOR YOU!
WELL, THEN, HOW ABOUT TAKING MY PLACE IN THE TOURNAMENT?

HA! I'M AFRAID NOT, MY GOOD SIR. I HAVE A DATE--WITH MY NEW MICROCOMPUTER.

MICROCOMPUTER! DON'T YOU EVER HAVE ANY FUN?
JEEZ!

WHY, I'LL BET ONE COULD EVEN WRITE A **PROGRAM** THAT WOULD ALLOW YOU TO TYPE A TERM PAPER **ELECTRONICALLY**. YOU COULD MAKE REVISIONS IN THE COMPUTER AND SAVE ALL THE DATA BEFORE PRINTING IT OUT!

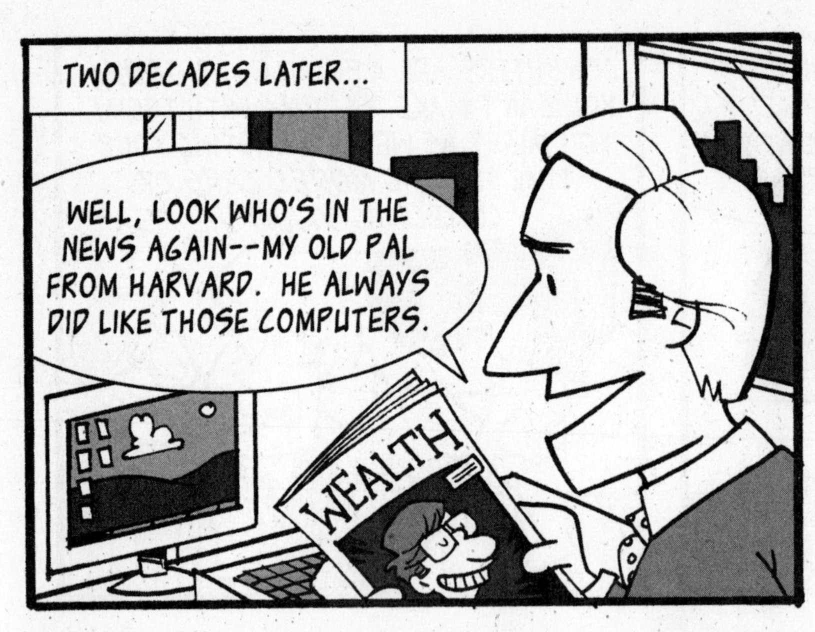
TWO DECADES LATER...
WELL, LOOK WHO'S IN THE NEWS AGAIN--MY OLD PAL FROM HARVARD. HE ALWAYS DID LIKE THOSE COMPUTERS.
WEALTH

HEY, DO YOU HAVE THAT MARKET ANALYSIS READY YET?

YOU BET--IT TOOK TWO SOLID WEEKS OF WORK, BUT IT'S FINALLY DONE AND SAVED RIGHT HERE IN MY TRUSTY COMPUTER.
WHY ARE YOU TALKING LIKE THAT?

NO REASON. JUST LET ME PRINT THAT OUT FOR YOU, AND--
CLICK!

OH NO!

WHAT? WHAT HAPPENED?
THE COMPUTER CRASHED AND I LOST EVERYTHING!
RUINED! MY PAPER IS RUINED!